MW00896793

101 Uplifting Stories for Seniors:

Delightful Easy-to-Read Short Stories to Stimulate Memory and Stir Heartwarming Nostalgia

Copyright © 2023 by Alex Clearwater

All rights reserved. No part of this publication may be reproduced, distributed, or transmitted in any form or by any means, including photocopying, recording, or other electronic or mechanical methods, without the prior written permission of the publisher, except in the case of brief quotations embodied in critical reviews and certain other noncommercial uses permitted by copyright law.

Published by Senior Smiles Press

First Edition: September 2023

Cover design by Frank Miller

Printed in the United States of America

This book is a work of fiction. Names, characters, places, and incidents either are the products of the author's imagination or are used fictitiously. Any resemblance to actual persons, living or dead, businesses, companies, events, or locales is entirely coincidental.

Contents

There's a certain magic that lives in memories—those golden moments that have a way of warming the heart, even years after they've passed. Each of us has a treasury of stories, both heard and lived, that carry the gentle power of nostalgia. And it's often in the simplest tales that we find the most profound truths.

These pages are filled with glimpses of bygone eras, days of vinyl records, handwritten letters, and Sunday drives in the family car. They're about first dances and last goodbyes, about the sweet melodies of youth and the quiet reflections of age. These stories, though specific in their details, carry universal emotions that will resonate with every generation.

You might find yourself reminded of an old friend, or perhaps you'll be transported back to a summer afternoon that you'd almost forgotten. Maybe you'll laugh, maybe you'll shed a tear, but our hope is that with each tale you read, you'll be reminded of the beauty and wonder that can be found in everyday life.

So, curl up in your favorite reading spot, be it a cozy armchair or a sunny nook by the window, and let's embark on this journey together. A journey that celebrates the past, cherishes the present, and welcomes the stories yet to be told.

Wishing you moments of quiet reflection and heartwarming smiles,

-Alex

Rediscovering the Charm of the 1950's

1. The Day Television Came Home

It was a day that young Tommy had been excited about for weeks. The living room was buzzing with more than just the chatter of his family members; it was buzzing with anticipation.

"We'll place it right there, next to the cabinet," Tommy's father, James, directed, as two delivery men carried a bulky object wrapped in cloth into the living room.

Tommy, along with his siblings Sarah and Michael, watched in awe as the object was placed down and the cloth removed, unveiling what could only be described as a technological marvel of its time—a television set.

"Wow!" Tommy's eyes widened as he took in the beauty of the 16-inch screen, housed in a wooden cabinet.

"Be careful, kids. This is more than just a box; it's a window to the world," James said, his voice filled with a mix of awe and gravitas.

As James fiddled with the dials and knobs, trying to get the antenna just right, Tommy's mother, Susan, brought in a tray of freshly baked cookies and lemonade, sensing that this was to be a momentous family occasion.

"Ah, got it!" James exclaimed as the screen flickered to life, displaying the black and white images of an evening news broadcast. The room fell silent for a moment, everyone entranced by the moving pictures and the crisp sound emanating from the set.

Just then, the screen transitioned to a local variety show, one that had been the talk of the town but which the Smith family had only ever heard on the radio. The host cracked a joke, and James laughed heartily, soon followed by the gleeful laughter of his family.

For Tommy, watching his father's face light up in that moment was like seeing him in a whole new light. His father, a hardworking man who rarely took a moment for himself, was genuinely happy.

The evening rolled on, but nobody was watching the clock. Even Susan, who usually insisted on early bedtimes, seemed to have forgotten about the hour. They were too engrossed, collectively lost in the world that their new television set opened up for them.

As the national anthem played to signify the end of the broadcasting day—something Tommy had only heard and never seen—the family stood up, almost on cue. It felt both solemn and joyous, as if they were part of a larger community they had just now discovered.

Before switching off the set, James turned to his family, his eyes twinkling. "You see, this isn't just entertainment. It's history in the making, and we're a part of it now."

That night, as Tommy lay in bed, he couldn't help but feel a sense of awe and wonder. The television had indeed become a new member of their family, one that would tell them stories, bring them news, and offer a shared experience that would bind them closer than ever before.

And so, the television found its permanent place not just in the corner of the Smith family's living room but in the corner of their hearts, marking the beginning of many more family moments to be cherished for a lifetime.

2. Elvis, The King of Rock 'n' Roll

Jenny knew she was taking a risk. Her parents were strait-laced, the kind of folks who believed that rock 'n' roll was the devil's music. But when she heard that Elvis Presley was going to be performing just a few towns over, she couldn't resist.

With her heart pounding, she snuck out of her bedroom window, her skirt and blouse carefully folded in a bag.

"Borrowed" was too innocent a word for what she did to her brother's bike, but she pedaled as if the wind were chasing her.

She got to the concert venue just in time, changed her clothes behind a tree, and blended into the crowd.

The air was thick with excitement, people milling around, waiting for the man of the hour. Jenny couldn't help but feel that she was about to witness history.

Finally, the lights dimmed, and a voice echoed through the speakers: "Ladies and Gentlemen, Elvis Presley!" The crowd erupted in screams and applause.

And there he was—Elvis, the King of Rock 'n' Roll. His opening chords reverberated through the arena, and the audience went wild. He wasn't just playing the guitar; he was commanding it, making it sing, shout, and practically dance.

Jenny felt like her heart would burst from her chest. It wasn't just the music—it was the raw energy, the charisma, the sheer life force that was Elvis. As he performed, the room seemed to spin, the crowd becoming one with the man and his music.

During a particularly energetic rendition of "Hound Dog," he shook his hips in that iconic way that made grown women faint and sent preachers to their pulpits. And for a fleeting moment, their eyes met. Jenny felt an electricity she had never felt before.

The concert seemed to end too soon, but its echo stayed with Jenny for a long time. She pedaled back home, her feet barely touching the pedals, her heart still dancing to the rhythm of the night.

Sneaking back into her room, she was met with a stroke of luck: her parents hadn't even noticed she was gone. As she lay in bed, a wide grin on her face, she knew that her life had just turned a page.

Jenny would go on to attend many more concerts, but nothing would ever compare to the magic of that night. It wasn't just an evening of music; it was the birth of a new era, a cultural revolution embodied by one man and his guitar. And Jenny could proudly say she was there when it all began.

Years later, when her own grandchildren asked her about the '50s, she would smile and say, "Kids, let me tell you about the time I saw the King."

In that moment, and for many moments afterward, Jenny knew she had not just witnessed history—she was a part of it. And as the years rolled on, every time she heard an Elvis song, she would close her eyes and be transported back to that one unforgettable night—the night she truly felt alive.

3. The Hula Hoop Craze

In a town where the most exciting event was the annual bake-off, the arrival of hula hoops was nothing short of revolutionary. Clara, a young mother, couldn't help but get swept up in the enthusiasm. It was contagious; you could feel it in the air, like the scent of fresh-cut grass or blooming flowers on the first day of spring.

When Clara heard that the local park was hosting a hula hoop contest, she knew it was something she couldn't miss. "This could be our own little slice of history, kids," she told her children, Tommy and Lucy, as she handed them each a shiny, new hula hoop.

The park was buzzing with activity on the day of the event. Families spread out on blankets, picnic baskets filled with sandwiches and lemonade by their side. The atmosphere was electric, like a fairground before the big ride started up.

Clara felt her heart swell with anticipation. "Look around, kids," she whispered, eyes twinkling. "Remember this day. It's something special."

Finally, the announcer's voice boomed through the makeshift speakers. "Ladies and Gentlemen, it's time for the great hula hoop showdown!"

The children lined up first, their hoops at the ready. Tommy was nervous; his palms were sweaty, making it hard to grip his hoop. But when he glanced over at his mom, her reassuring smile melted his jitters away.

The whistle blew, and the hoops started rolling. Some stumbled and fumbled, but not Tommy and Lucy. They spun their hoops like pros, carried by the cheers and the adrenaline. The contest became a blur of color and motion, kids and adults alike lost in the simple joy of a plastic ring.

As the competition winded down, the crowd gathered around the final contestants. Clara had made it to the adult finals. Her heart was pounding, not from the exertion but from the sheer excitement of it all.

Another whistle, another round. Clara's hoop seemed to spin effortlessly around her waist, as if enchanted. She looked out into the crowd, locking eyes with her children. In that moment, she felt invincible.

When the whistle blew to signify the end, Clara was declared the winner amidst a roar of applause. As she stood there, hula hoop in hand and children by her side, she felt like she was part of something much bigger—a collective experience that would be etched into the memories of everyone present.

"That was amazing, Mom!" Tommy exclaimed, hugging her tightly.

"Yeah, you were awesome!" Lucy joined in, her eyes shining with pride.

As they packed up their picnic and their prized hoops, Clara knew this was a day they would talk about for years to come. It wasn't just a contest; it was a snapshot of an era, a testament to the simple joys that defined their lives in that seemingly distant yet vividly memorable time.

When Clara's grandchildren would one day ask her what it was like growing up in the '50s, she would smile, pick up an old hula hoop she'd kept all those years, and say, "Let me show you how we rolled."

4. Sock Hops and Poodle Skirts

Patty's heart raced with a mix of anticipation and nerves as she stared into her closet, sifting through a sea of fabric and patterns. This wasn't just any night; it was the night of her first sock hop, and every detail had to be perfect.

"Sweetie, are you almost ready?" Her mother's voice called from downstairs.

"Just a minute, Mom!" Patty finally pulled out the piece de resistance: a powder pink poodle skirt she and her mom had spent weeks sewing together. It was adorned with a small, fluffy poodle near the hem, a whimsical touch that brought Patty immense joy.

She slipped into the skirt, paired it with a crisp, white blouse, and added a scarf for good measure. A quick look in the mirror confirmed what she already felt: tonight was going to be magical.

Patty raced downstairs, her bobby socks whispering against the carpet. Her mom beamed at her, "Oh, you look just darling!"

Her dad was at the ready with the camera. "Say cheese!" he commanded, capturing the moment in black and white, a snapshot of youthful exuberance in a bygone era.

They arrived at the high school gymnasium, which had been transformed into a pastel paradise complete with paper streamers and a jukebox. The air was thick with the scent of hairspray and freshly polished floors.

Patty felt a rush of adrenaline as the first chords of "Rock Around the Clock" filled the room. Kids in loafers and bobby socks swarmed the dance floor, carried away by the beat.

As she timidly stepped onto the dance floor, Patty felt a gentle tap on her shoulder. It was Tommy, her longtime crush. His hair was impeccably styled in a modest pompadour, and he was wearing a varsity jacket that made him look like he'd stepped right out of a magazine.

"May I have this dance?" he asked, a nervous twinkle in his eyes.

Her heart soared. "I'd be delighted," she managed to say, even though her heart was pounding so loudly she was sure the whole gym could hear it.

As they danced, Patty felt like she was floating on air. Tommy was a good dancer, easy to follow, and it felt as though they were in their own little world. Around them, friends and classmates laughed, twirled, and jived, but Patty only had eyes for Tommy.

As the night progressed, Patty realized that she wasn't just part of a dance; she was part of a cultural phenomenon that defined her generation. The sock hop wasn't just a night of fun; it was a communal experience, a break from the routines and restrictions of everyday life.

Finally, the last song of the evening began to play, a slow tune that seemed to echo the collective sentiment of not wanting the night to end. Tommy held Patty a little closer as they swayed, and for a brief moment, everything felt perfect.

When the music eventually stopped, and the lights came on, Patty felt a sense of melancholy mixed with gratitude. She looked around, capturing the faces, the colors, and the atmosphere in her mind, like a mental photograph she'd revisit for years to come.

As they pulled into the driveway, Patty couldn't help but feel a bittersweet pang. The night had come to an end, but the experience was etched into her heart. She knew she would return to the sock hop next month, but there was something singular about this first time, something irreplaceable.

"Thanks, Mom, Dad," Patty said as she stepped out of the car, "Tonight was really special."

Her dad grinned, "Well, kiddo, life is full of special moments. Tonight was one of them, and there'll be many more to come."

Her mom added, "And maybe, one day, you'll tell your own kids about your first sock hop."

Patty nodded, "I just might." But as she headed towards her room, she took a detour to the living room where the family record player sat. Gently, she placed the needle on her favorite Elvis record. As the music filled the room, Patty twirled alone, her poodle skirt fanning out around her.

In that quiet moment, Patty felt like she carried a piece of the '50s with her, a slice of history that was entirely her own. And so, in the dim glow of her living room, she danced—not for her classmates, not for Tommy, but for herself.

For Patty, this private dance was a promise, a commitment to keep embracing the joys and wonders that life would surely bring.

And though she didn't know it yet, this youthful resolve would empower her through the decades to come, becoming a story she'd recount not as a distant memory but as the beginning of her lifelong journey.

5. The Drive-In Experience

Alan had been planning this for weeks. The drive-in theater had just released its movie schedule for the month, and the featured film this weekend was "Breakfast at Tiffany's."

It was perfect—romantic but not overly sentimental, classy but accessible. In his mind, it was the ideal choice for a first date with Karen, the young lady he'd been smitten with since their chance meeting at a mutual friend's party.

"Ready to go?" he asked, looking at Karen who had just climbed into the passenger seat of his Chevrolet Impala.

"Absolutely!" she replied, her eyes twinkling with excitement.

The drive to the theater was filled with small talk and a couple of awkward silences, but both felt an inexplicable magic in the air. They finally arrived at the drive-in and found a spot that offered a good view of the large outdoor screen.

"Do you want anything from the snack bar? Popcorn? Soda?" Alan asked, flipping a few coins in his hand.

"A soda would be nice, thanks," Karen said with a smile.

As Alan left for the snack bar, Karen looked around. The other cars were filling up quickly with couples, families, and groups of friends.

She felt a wave of nostalgia, even in the present moment, knowing that this was an experience unique to this era—one that she'd probably tell her future kids about.

Alan returned with two sodas and a bag of popcorn, and they both settled in. The movie began, and the familiar face of Audrey Hepburn illuminated the screen, larger than life yet remarkably intimate in the setting of a drive-in.

They sipped their sodas and shared popcorn, occasionally stealing glances at each other. As the movie played on, both were deeply engrossed, not just in the unfolding story but also in the unfolding possibilities between them.

Then it happened, the iconic scene where Hepburn's character sings "Moon River." Alan took that as his cue. Slowly, almost cautiously, he reached over and took Karen's hand.

She looked at him and smiled, her eyes mirroring the silver screen's moonlight. It was as if time froze, capturing the essence of youthful love, hope, and an era defined by its untamed optimism.

As the credits rolled and patrons started their cars, Alan and Karen remained seated, still holding hands.

"That was lovely," Karen finally broke the silence, "this whole evening was just... lovely."

"I'm glad you enjoyed it," Alan replied, feeling a mixture of relief and elation.

As they drove back, the car seemed to glide effortlessly, as if powered by the night's enchantment. Both knew they were part of something larger—a cultural tapestry that extended beyond movies and cars, into the very way love stories unfolded in those years.

Years later, whenever Alan and Karen would pass an old drive-in, converted into something less magical—a shopping center, perhaps—they'd look at each other and smile. No words were needed; they both knew they had been part of an era when romance flickered on massive outdoor screens, and first loves could truly be larger than life.

Though times would change, their drive-in experience remained a touchstone, a sweet memory preserved in the amber of a bygone era, treasured all the more for its fleeting impermanence.

6. The Polio Vaccine

The weight of anticipation hung in the air like a dense fog as Mary waited with her children, Sarah and Jack, in the clinic's small waiting room. The Salk vaccine had finally been released to the public, and today was the day they'd receive their first dose.

"Mom, why are there so many people here?" young Jack asked, tugging on Mary's dress.

Mary looked down at him, smiling reassuringly. "Because, sweetheart, today is a very special day. Today is the day we start to beat polio."

For Mary and her husband, Tom, the fight against polio was deeply personal. Tom's younger brother had contracted the disease years earlier and had spent much of his life confined to a wheelchair.

Mary remembered that time—the fear, the uncertainty, the way neighbors would cross the street to avoid them. She shook off the haunting memories and looked at Sarah and Jack, their faces brimming with youthful innocence. Never again, she thought.

Finally, the nurse called their names. "Mary, Sarah, Jack, you're up."

They followed her into a small room where Dr. Williams was waiting with a tray of syringes. The doctor's face was tired but elated, as if he too knew the significance of this moment.

"Alright, who wants to go first?" Dr. Williams asked, looking at Sarah and Jack.

"I will," Sarah volunteered bravely, rolling up her sleeve.

As the needle went in, Mary felt her own tension release. This was more than just a shot; it was a shot at a future free from the crippling fear of a merciless disease.

Soon it was Jack's turn, then Mary's. The doctor placed a small bandage on each of their arms and handed them a card. "Make sure to come back for the second dose," he reminded them.

As they left the clinic, Mary could see the sun breaking through the clouds, casting a golden light on the faces of everyone waiting their turn for the vaccine. She felt a renewed sense of community, united by the collective relief and hope the vaccine represented.

Later, Mary recounted the day's events to Tom. As he listened, his eyes filled with tears. "You know," he said, choking up, "I can't help but think of my brother. How different things might have been for him."

"Yes," Mary nodded, "but just think of how different things will be for Sarah and Jack. And for all the other children, too."

Tom took her hand, squeezing it tightly. In that moment, they both knew they were part of something much larger than themselves—a seminal moment that would be etched into the annals of history, a moment that defined a generation and changed the course of public health forever.

7. The Kitchen Revolution

Linda had spent countless hours standing over the sink, hands wrinkled from soap and water, scrubbing away the remnants of family meals. Today, however, was different—today was revolutionary.

"Okay, honey, stand back. Let's see if this thing actually works," said John, Linda's husband, as he crouched in front of their brand new dishwasher.

"Is it hooked up correctly?" Linda asked, holding her breath.

John pressed a button, and with a gentle hum, the machine sprung to life. Their kids, Nancy and Tom, ran into the kitchen, curious to see the new contraption their parents were so excited about.

"Mom, Dad, what's going on?" Tom asked, staring at the dishwasher.

"Kids, this is more than just a machine. This is freedom—freedom from endless dishwashing!" Linda declared, unable to contain her glee.

Nancy and Tom exchanged puzzled glances but shrugged it off; their mom was happy, so it must be good.

Over the next few days, Linda felt like a weight had been lifted. She could spend more time with the kids, more time reading, or simply more time sitting and enjoying a cup of coffee. The dishwasher might have been a small appliance, but it felt like a huge step forward.

As the neighbors heard about Linda's newfound liberation, one by one, dishwashers began appearing in kitchens up and down the block. During weekend get-togethers, the conversation inevitably turned to the wonders of modern appliances. They all agreed: Life would never be the same.

One evening, Linda gathered the family around the kitchen table for dinner. "Guess what? Mrs. Johnson got a dishwasher too! Can you believe it? The whole neighborhood is changing."

John chuckled, "Well, I guess we started a little revolution, didn't we?"

Linda looked around at her family—her husband, her children, and their spotless plates—and realized that this was about more than just making her life easier.

It was a moment in time, one that signaled change not just in her home, but in homes everywhere. And although it was a small, everyday thing, she knew it was a milestone that would be passed down through generations.

As they finished dinner, Tom asked, "So what's next, Mom? A robot to do the laundry?"

Everyone laughed, but Linda caught John's eye and they both knew that whatever came next, they'd welcome it—with open arms and an open heart.

8. Disneyland's Opening Day

For little Billy, the idea of Disneyland felt almost too magical to be real. He had heard it on TV, seen it in newspapers, and couldn't believe that the gates to "The Happiest Place On Earth" were about to open. Today was the day, and Billy couldn't be more thrilled.

"Come on, kids, into the car! We've got a long drive ahead," hollered Dad from the driveway.

"Did you bring the camera, Helen?" he asked his wife.

"Check! And I've packed sandwiches and lemonade," she replied.

As they drove toward Anaheim, Billy and his younger sister, Sarah, couldn't contain their excitement. Their faces were practically glued to the car windows as they looked out for signs pointing the way to Disneyland.

Finally, they arrived, and the atmosphere was electrifying. Flags were waving, music was playing, and the smell of popcorn filled the air. This was the moment they had all been waiting for.

"Remember, this isn't just an amusement park; this is a piece of history," Dad said as they stepped through the turnstile.

The family roamed through the park, marveling at the sights. Frontierland, Tomorrowland, Fantasyland—it was like walking through different worlds.

Billy's eyes widened as they reached the Dumbo ride. "Can we go, Dad? Please?"

"Of course, sport," Dad replied with a chuckle.

As the ride lifted off, Billy felt like he was flying. The view from above was a sea of smiling faces, a vision of pure joy.

Soon, they were watching the Jungle Cruise boats, sailing through a 'dangerous' jungle filled with mechanical animals. Sarah screamed in delight when they encountered the "headhunter."

The day was drawing to an end, but the biggest surprise was yet to come—Tinker Bell's flight over Sleeping Beauty Castle as fireworks lit up the night sky.

"Wow, that's real pixie dust," Sarah gasped.

Billy looked at his family—their faces lit by the sparkle of fireworks—and knew this was a memory they'd cherish forever.

"It's like a dream come true," Mom whispered to Dad, who squeezed her hand in agreement.

As they left the park, Billy looked back one more time, burning the image of the glowing castle into his memory. Though he was young, he understood that they had been part of something monumental, a grand opening that would make history.

Years later, as Disneyland expanded and evolved, Billy would return with his own kids, and eventually his grandchildren.

Each visit was a reminder of that opening day, a day that had not just been about rides and attractions but a collective moment of shared happiness and wonder.

And so, that day became more than just an outing for a young boy and his family; it became part of the emotional tapestry of an entire nation. A place where dreams could come true, and where every visitor—even a little boy named Billy—became part of "The Happiest Place On Earth."

Decades would pass, but the magic of that first day never wore off. Each time Billy heard the familiar tunes of Disney songs, he'd be instantly transported back to that extraordinary day in 1955—a day that defined not just his childhood but the dreams and aspirations of generations to come.

9. The '55 Chevy: A Car for the Ages

For 19-year-old Tommy, the path to adulthood was not college degrees or fancy jobs; it was four wheels and an engine. And not just any engine, but the V8 nestled under the hood of a 1955 Chevrolet. It was the epitome of the American dream, at least for a young man who felt the call of the open road.

"Tommy, time for dinner," his mother called from the kitchen.

"Be right there, Ma," Tommy replied, as he put down the latest issue of "Hot Rod Magazine," where a '55 Chevy took center stage.

Working two jobs—at the local grocery and the gas station—Tommy saved every nickel and dime. His friends were skeptical. "Why don't you get a beater car first?" they'd say. But Tommy was resolute. A '55 Chevy was what he wanted, and he wouldn't settle for less.

"Counting your riches again?" his dad would jest as Tommy added to his car fund jar each week.

"You'll see, Dad," Tommy would reply, a spark in his eyes.

Months passed, and the jar filled up, coin by laborious coin. Then, the day came. A local dealer had a '55 Chevy for sale, and Tommy was finally ready. Heart pounding, palms sweaty, he handed over the money and got the keys in return. It was a moment as significant as any graduation.

"Look at you, son! A man with his car," his dad exclaimed, patting him on the back as they stood in front of their home, the Chevy parked on the driveway.

Tommy revved the engine, and it was like music—a symphony of horsepower and freedom. His mother, holding back tears of pride, insisted on taking the first family ride. They all piled in, and Tommy steered the Chevy around town, every turn a statement, every honk a celebration.

As days turned into weeks, the Chevy became more than just a car. It was Tommy's passport to a new world. Whether it was driving his date to the prom or helping his dad bring home lumber for a weekend project, the car was an extension of himself—a metallic, chrome-laden version of the American Dream.

The freedom that Chevy offered him was transformative. Gone were the days of catching rides or waiting for the bus. Now, the world felt smaller, more accessible.

His weekends were no longer confined to his small town; coastal drives and big city visits were now within reach.

And as the years rolled on, that '55 Chevy became a part of family folklore. Tommy would eventually go to college, get married, and have kids of his own. The Chevy? It was passed down to the next generation—a rolling testament to the power of dreams and the persistence to realize them.

Decades later, Tommy would look at old photos, his grown kids by his side, and say, "That car taught me what it means to be free."

With a gleam in his eye, reminiscent of that 19-year-old who once yearned for the open road, Tommy would tell them, "Kids, never underestimate the power of dreams. And never, ever settle for anything less than you deserve."

In years to come, every time one of Tommy's descendants would sit behind the wheel of an old or new Chevy, they would be reminded of the dreams, diligence, and spirit of freedom that defined not just a young man named Tommy, but a generation fueled by ambition and hope.

10. The Rotary Phone: A Household Marvel

The Thompson family was buzzing with excitement on a Saturday morning, a feeling that even surpassed the joy of Saturday morning cartoons. Today, they were joining the modern world—they were getting a rotary phone installed.

"Alright, kids, let's clear the living room table. The phone man will be here any minute," said Jane, the Thompson matriarch, wringing her apron in anticipation.

And arrive he did, in a crisp uniform and a toolbox in hand. Within half an hour, there it was—a gleaming rotary phone sitting like a crown jewel in the heart of the Thompson home. Mr. Thompson, usually reserved, was the first to break the silence.

"Who wants to make the first call?" he asked, beaming.

Little Susie's hand shot up, "Can I call Grandma?"

"Go ahead, sweetie," her mom encouraged.

Fumbling at first, Susie dialed each number carefully, round and round the dial went. Then, the magical sound of ringing on the other end. "Hello, Grandma! It's Susie! We have a phone at home now!"

Laughter and smiles filled the room as Grandma's warm voice echoed from the receiver. Next, it was Bobby's turn. He called his friend Timmy down the street to plan a bike race for the afternoon. Even Mrs. Thompson had a sentimental conversation with her sister, who lived in another state.

But the real showstopper was Mr. Thompson, who dialed a long-distance number with an air of gravitas. "That's your Uncle Bill. He's in California, kids. CALIFORNIA!"

The room hushed as the call went through. The children's eyes widened, imagining their voices traveling across mountains and deserts to reach Uncle Bill. And when the connection was made, and they heard his surprised voice, it was like touching a piece of the vast, endless sky.

In the days that followed, the rotary phone became the hub of the household, ushering in news both grand and mundane. Birthday wishes were sung, holiday plans were made, and aunts and uncles gave life advice, all through that marvelous device.

Years later, smartphones and video calls would make the rotary phone seem like a relic. But for the Thompsons, and families like them, it was a gateway to a bigger world.

It connected them to far-flung loved ones and turned ordinary days into series of small, beautiful moments—each call a celebration, each conversation a treasured memory.

As the children grew up and told their kids about the magic of that first rotary phone, it served as a reminder of a simpler, yet extraordinary time.

The rotary phone may have been a piece of technology, but for the Thompson family, it was the hearth around which they gathered, sharing stories and love, one dial at a time.

11. The Ice Cream Truck's Melody

It was one of those hot summer afternoons when the air seemed almost syrupy, and even the crickets were too lazy to chirp. But then, like a wizard casting a spell over the neighborhood, the jingle of the ice cream truck broke the heat-induced trance.

As if cued by the magical tune, children burst from their homes like popcorn kernels in a hot pan. Dressed in mismatched bathing suits and sporting grass-stained knees, they ran toward the source of the music. It wasn't just any music; it was the anthem of summer.

Billy's dad, Jim, who was normally engrossed in his woodworking, wiped the sawdust off his hands and reached for his wallet. "Hold on, champ. Let's get you some ice cream," he called out, unable to resist the allure.

Molly, who was in her forties but still the neighborhood's reigning jump rope champion, sauntered over with a smile. "You know, when I was your age, that truck was the highlight of my summer too," she said, eyes twinkling.

Even Grandma Davis, who rarely ventured out of her porch rocker, was lured by the enchanting melody. "Well, I suppose one ice cream sandwich won't ruin my diet," she muttered, but her eager steps betrayed her real feelings.

When the truck finally rolled to a stop, a cheerful man named Larry popped his head out, fully aware that he was the pied piper of this suburban symphony. "Alright, kiddos, what'll it be today?"

The answers varied—snow cones, ice cream sandwiches, rocket popsicles—but the result was the same. Faces lit up, conversation flowed, and for a few minutes, age didn't matter. Kids and adults alike licked their treats, each sugary bite dissolving the day's worries and the decade's complexities.

As the truck pulled away, leaving behind the echo of its jingle, everyone returned to their homes, their summer sanctuaries. But something had changed. A sense of unity lingered in the air, sweeter than any ice cream.

Years later, hearing a similar jingle from a modern ice cream truck, the grown-up children would be instantly transported back to those carefree summer days.

Days when the most critical decision was choosing between a Fudgsicle and a Drumstick. Days when the neighborhood felt like one big family, all thanks to the ice cream truck's melody.

The ice cream truck didn't just sell frozen treats; it sold joy, connection, and fleeting moments that became lasting memories. It was a simple thing, really, but sometimes the simplest things define an era, making it forever memorable.

12. The Birth of the Barbie Doll

The air was crisp and tinged with the scent of pine and cinnamon as Judy woke up to the thrill of Christmas morning. Her feet hit the cold floor, instantly energized by the thought of what lay under the tree. "Mom! Dad! Wake up; it's Christmas!" she called, bounding down the stairs two at a time.

Her parents, Lisa and Tom, already up and sipping coffee, chuckled. "Alright, princess, let's see what Santa brought you," Tom said, setting his cup down and making his way to the tree.

With paper flying, Judy tore through her gifts—new crayons, a puzzle, and a hula hoop. But it was the last box that caught her eye. Carefully wrapped in shimmering silver paper, it seemed to promise something extraordinary.

Her hands trembled as she opened it, revealing the elegant figure of a woman dressed in a stylish black-and-white swimsuit. "She's beautiful!" Judy exclaimed, her eyes lighting up like the Christmas tree beside her.

"That, my dear, is a Barbie doll," Lisa said, beaming at her daughter's delight. "She's very special— one of the first of her kind."

Tom nodded. "She's more than just a doll, Judy. She can be anything she wants to be—a fashion model today, maybe a doctor or astronaut tomorrow. Just like you."

Judy was entranced. Unlike her baby dolls, this one seemed different, as if brimming with possibilities yet to be imagined. It wasn't just a toy; it was a statement—a declaration that girls could aspire to be more than what society told them to be.

As the years rolled by, Barbie did indeed assume many roles in Judy's life. From makeshift runways on the living room floor to 'hospital rooms' set up on the kitchen table, the plastic figure was a constant companion in Judy's ever-expanding world…

Years later, Judy found herself sipping coffee on a different Christmas morning, this time watching her own daughter tearing through wrapping paper with the same youthful exuberance she once had.

When her daughter opened her own Barbie doll, Judy was instantly transported back to her childhood home, to the scent of pine and cinnamon, and to the tree twinkling with lights.

"Wow, Mom, she's beautiful!" her daughter exclaimed, echoing the very words Judy had uttered years ago.

Judy smiled, feeling a sense of continuity that was deeply comforting. "She is, sweetheart. Just like you."

As her daughter dashed off to introduce Barbie to her other toys, Judy caught her husband's eye and they shared a knowing smile. For a moment, she was a child again, reminded of her parents' love and the simple joys that made childhood magical.

13. Saturday Morning Cartoons

It was a Saturday morning like no other. At least that's how it felt for Tommy, Lisa, and their younger brother, Mikey. They had heard whispers in the schoolyard all week—"This Saturday, cartoons all morning!"

Their mom was more lenient with TV time on weekends. "No schoolwork today, so you kids enjoy," she said, setting down a plate of buttered toast and orange juice on the coffee table.

Tommy took control of the dial—no remote controls in those days—and switched the black-and-white set to the channel they'd all agreed upon.

First up, "The Flintstones." Tommy and Lisa were fascinated by the prehistoric but oddly modern world of Fred and Wilma, while Mikey giggled at the dinosaur pets. The room filled with their laughter and the light scent of Mom's brewing coffee from the kitchen.

As the credits rolled, Lisa wondered aloud, "What's next?"

"Bugs Bunny!" Tommy announced. A sense of pure excitement vibrated through the room.

Sure enough, the lovable rabbit appeared on screen, outwitting Elmer Fudd in his usual, hilarious fashion. Tommy imitated Bugs' Brooklyn accent, making Mikey laugh so hard he nearly spit out his orange juice.

Throughout the morning, they watched one cartoon after another. "Popeye the Sailor," "Yogi Bear," "Rocky and Bullwinkle"—each show brought them into a new, fantastical world, far removed from school, chores, or the everyday mundanities of childhood.

It was just pure, undiluted fun, the kind that makes you forget about time, that fills the room with the kind of laughter and silliness that only kids really understand.

When the clock hands eventually reached noon, Mom reappeared. "Alright, kids. How about we get some fresh air?" she suggested.

They groaned but complied. Yet, as they put on their jackets and headed outside, they kept talking about their favorite parts—how Bugs had tricked Elmer again, how Fred Flintstone's car worked with feet, and whether Popeye's spinach could really make you strong.

Outside, the sun was higher in the sky, and the neighborhood kids were already engaged in a game of stickball in the street. Tommy, Lisa, and Mikey joined in, and as Tommy swung a successful hit, he shouted his best Bugs Bunny, "Ain't I a stinker?" making everyone burst into laughter.

As the afternoon unfolded, with games of stickball, tag, and jump-rope, the morning's magic lingered. For those few hours in front of the TV, they had been adventurers, time travelers, and explorers in worlds they could only dream of.

It was a simple, singular joy, the kind that feels big in small lives. Even without saying it, they knew they shared something special that morning, a cozy cocoon of childhood where the outside world could wait a little longer.

14. The Day Roger Bannister Broke the Four-Minute Mile

Tom sat fidgeting on the living room floor, watching his father, Jack, fine-tune the dial on their old tabletop radio.

The hum of static gave way to a crisp British voice saying, "Ladies and gentlemen, we are moments away from Roger Bannister's attempt at breaking the four-minute mile."

"Sit still, Tommy. You'll want to remember this," Jack advised, his eyes narrowing as if trying to see the event through the radio itself.

Tom adjusted his sitting posture and looked at the black-and-white photo of his dad in a track uniform, placed prominently on the mantelpiece. Jack had been a decent runner in his day, but nothing close to what they were about to hear.

Finally, the announcer's voice broke the silence, "And he's off!" For the next few minutes, the small living room was filled with the play-by-play of Roger Bannister running the laps.

Each description of his pace, his form, his determination was like a brushstroke painting an invisible image in the air—Jack and Tom leaning in as if they could will Bannister to go faster. "Final stretch!" the announcer practically screamed. "He's done it! Three minutes, fifty-nine point four seconds!"

Jack whooped and grabbed Tom's shoulder, giving it a joyous squeeze. "He broke it, Tommy! Broke it!"

A week later, Tom found himself in the backyard wearing his father's old track shoes, which were a few sizes too big. His course was nothing more than a loop around their property, marked by garden stones and a gnarled apple tree. Jack stood with a stopwatch, a smile covering his face.

"Ready, set, go!" Jack shouted.

Tom's initial steps were awkward in the oversized shoes, but he soon found his rhythm. He rounded the apple tree, his lungs burning but his heart buoyant. When he crossed his makeshift finish line, Jack clicked the stopwatch.

"Five minutes and twenty-one seconds," Jack announced, but the numbers didn't matter.

That evening, Tom placed the stopwatch on the mantelpiece, next to his dad's old track photo. Neither of them spoke about it, but both understood. It wasn't just a moment in history they had listened to; it was a moment that had trotted through their living room, laced up its shoes, and sprinted right into their lives.

15. Meeting Marilyn Monroe: A G.I.'s Dream

"Congratulations, Private Johnson. You're the lucky dog!" Sergeant Miller slapped him on the back, handing over a crumpled letter. It was an invitation. Henry had won the lottery to meet Marilyn Monroe during her USO tour.

His boots were dusted, and his uniform pressed to an inch of its life. Standing in line with a dozen other soldiers, Henry felt a ball of nerves and excitement churning in his stomach. "This is the sort of story I'll tell my grandkids," he thought.

Marilyn Monroe walked onto the makeshift stage like a vision—a cascade of platinum blonde curls, a radiant smile, and a white dress that seemed sewn from moonbeams. The soldiers erupted in applause and whistles, and Henry felt like his heart might burst right there.

Then the moment arrived. One by one, the soldiers approached her for a brief chat and a photograph. When Henry's turn came, he was a bundle of nerves, a stark contrast to the poised goddess before him.

"Hello, soldier. What's your name?" she said, her voice every bit as enchanting as he'd imagined.

"Henry, ma'am."

"You can call me Marilyn, Henry."

He could barely find his voice, but somehow he managed to say, "It's an honor, Marilyn. My sister's a huge fan. Could you autograph this for her?"

He handed over a small notebook and a pen, and Marilyn graciously scribbled her name and a little message. Then they took a photograph, her arm lightly resting on his shoulder.

Years later, that faded photograph would sit framed on Henry's nightstand. But it wasn't the glamor or the fame that he remembered most.

It was the brief flicker in Marilyn's eyes, a momentary shadow that told him she was just as human as anyone else.

Henry cherished that brief encounter, not for the touch of stardom it brought into his life, but for the grounding realization that underneath the makeup and the dazzling dresses, icons were made of the same stuff as the rest of us—flesh, bone, and a hunger for genuine connection.

Whenever he told the story, it wasn't the awe of meeting Marilyn Monroe he wanted to pass on; it was the warmth of that human connection, a single authentic moment that illuminated, however briefly, the lives of two people who existed worlds apart.

16. Little League Dreams

The year was 1952, and Billy couldn't have been more excited. It was Little League season, and that meant one thing: a summer of endless baseball.

This was the America of the 1950s, when every young boy seemed to have a bat and ball in his hands, and the smell of fresh-cut grass was as much a part of the landscape as white picket fences.

Billy's father, John, was equally excited. Recently back from the war, he was embracing his role as a dad with gusto. He spent every evening with Billy, tossing balls in the backyard, teaching him the basics of pitching, and refining his swing.

The two of them would listen to the crackling radio broadcasts of big league games as the sun dipped below the horizon, dreaming of one day making it big.

For weeks, Billy practiced with his teammates on a field that was as American as apple pie—a simple diamond-shaped patch of earth, bounded by trees and the laughter of children. Finally, it was time for the championship game, and the whole neighborhood seemed to have turned out.

Fathers with fedoras, mothers in their Sunday dresses, and siblings whooping and hollering filled the makeshift bleachers.

Billy was nervous; he was the closing pitcher. As he walked onto the mound, he looked over and saw his father giving him a thumbs-up. The energy was palpable.

Then, the moment arrived. Bases loaded, two outs, and the pressure was on. Billy took a deep breath, wound up, and released. The ball sailed through the air, landing squarely in the catcher's mitt—a strike. The crowd erupted; they had won the championship!

In the jubilant huddle that followed, trophies handed out like candy, Billy glanced over at his father, who was grinning from ear to ear. Their eyes met, and in that silent exchange, an entire world of feelings seemed to pass—love, pride, and the pure, undiluted joy of the game.

And so, as the sun set on that perfect summer day, the smell of victory mingled with the aroma of fresh popcorn and hot dogs, sealing a moment in time neither Billy nor his father would ever forget. For them, it wasn't just a game; it was a piece of a dream that tasted as sweet as victory itself.

17. The Crooning of Frank Sinatra

In a softly lit room filled with the lingering scent of her favorite lavender candle, Marie placed an old vinyl record onto the turntable.

As the needle met the grooves, the rich voice of Frank Sinatra filled the air. Her husband, Richard, extended his hand, inviting her to a dance they had done countless times over the decades.

"Remember the first time we danced to Sinatra, Marie?" Richard asked, gently leading her around their small living room.

"Of course," she replied, her eyes twinkling. "How could I forget? It was 1954, at the Autumn Ball."

They were young then, their entire lives stretching out before them like an open road. Marie wore a red satin dress, and Richard had slicked back his hair in true greaser style.

As Sinatra crooned "Young at Heart," they found themselves lost in each other's eyes for the very first time. They both knew, even then, that this was a love that would last.

Over the years, Sinatra's songs became the soundtrack of their lives together—from the birth of their children to the challenges and triumphs they weathered side by side.

The lyrics to "My Way" played softly in the background when Richard retired, and Marie had hummed "Strangers in the Night" as they celebrated their 50th anniversary.

But tonight was different. There were no grand celebrations or milestones to mark. It was just an ordinary evening, and yet, it felt extraordinarily special.

As Sinatra's voice sang "Fly Me to the Moon," Richard pulled Marie closer, savoring the feel of her hand in his and the love that had only grown deeper over the years.

As the music came to a gentle end, they stood there for a moment, arms wrapped around each other, feeling the profound sense of comfort and happiness that only years of being together could bring.

They didn't need to say it out loud; their hearts knew the truth—that they were indeed lucky to have lived a life so beautifully soundtracked by Sinatra's timeless tunes.

The record player hummed softly, ready for another spin, and they realized that some songs truly never end.

18. Queen Elizabeth II's Coronation: A Family United

It was a crisp morning on June 2, 1953, and inside the Johnsons' living room, a sense of wonder filled the air. Sarah Johnson was meticulously arranging the snacks—tea, biscuits, and little finger sandwiches—while her husband, Bill, fiddled with their brand-new television set. He was trying to get the antenna just right to catch the live broadcast of Queen Elizabeth II's coronation.

"Alright, kids, gather 'round!" Sarah called out, ushering in Tim and Emily, who were eager but puzzled. "Why is it so special to watch a queen from another country, Mom?" asked Emily, her eyes wide with curiosity.

"Ah, well," began Sarah, "our family has roots in England, my dear. Your great-great-grandparents sailed from Liverpool to start a new life here."

Just then, the snowy static on the screen cleared, revealing the image of Queen Elizabeth II, looking regal and composed. The whole family fell silent, captivated by the grandeur unfolding miles away but beamed right into their humble living room.

Even Tim, who had the restlessness of any eight-year-old, was fixed to the screen, particularly interested in the Archbishop and the scepter.

"Wow, so that's a real queen?" Tim finally spoke, breaking the silence.

"Indeed, it is," Bill answered, his voice tinged with pride. "And this is a big part of world history we're watching."

After the broadcast ended, the kids couldn't contain their questions. "What's that crown made of?" "Do we have a family crest?" "Can we visit England one day?"

Sarah smiled, retrieving an old, dusty photo album from a bookshelf. "Here's something to answer some of your questions," she said, showing them pictures of relatives in front of British landmarks, some wearing military uniforms.

At that moment, something shifted inside that living room. This wasn't just an international event they had witnessed; it was a portal to their own past, an unspoken yet palpable connection to a lineage that seemed so distant yet suddenly so near.

Weeks later, the Johnsons found themselves at the local library, researching their ancestry and even planning a 'family roots' trip to England.

And while the grandeur of the coronation faded from the news, its echo lived on in the Johnson home, immortalized in a simple family photo taken that day, their faces lit by the glow of history, curiosity, and a newfound sense of who they were.

19. The Rise of Fast Food

Margaret pulled up to the parking lot in her weathered station wagon, her husband, Jack, at her side, and three excited kids in the backseat—Ellen, Tommy, and little Susie. "Mom, is this the place where the burgers come really, really fast?" Tommy asked, his eyes as big as saucers.

"Yes, it is!" Margaret said, equally thrilled. Fast food was still a new phenomenon, and this was their town's first-ever fast-food joint. "A meal in minutes—that's what they say!"

As they walked in, the smell of sizzling burgers and fresh fries filled the air. The kids pressed their faces against the glass counter, marveling at the shiny metallic surfaces and the staff in crisp white uniforms.

"Can we have milkshakes, too?" Susie's voice quivered with excitement.

"Of course," Jack chuckled, ordering a family feast. Just as promised, in a matter of minutes, trays laden with burgers, fries, and milkshakes arrived at their red and white booth.

With the first bite, their faces lit up. "This is amazing!" Ellen declared, her teenage nonchalance momentarily suspended. "It's so... juicy!"

Margaret had a more complex reaction. The burger was delicious, no doubt. But as she looked at her family, she thought of the afternoons spent rolling dough for homemade apple pie and the hours by the stove making her mother's spaghetti sauce. Would all that vanish in this new age of instant everything?

But then she noticed something—Jack was showing Tommy how to balance a spoon on his nose, Ellen was making funny faces with ketchup, and Susie was doodling with a straw wrapper, all while slurping her milkshake. The setting had changed, the food had come in record time, but the joy, the togetherness, the family—those were as they had always been.

When they left, each child carried a small toy that came with their meal—a tiny memento from their first foray into fast food.

And while the milkshakes melted and the toys eventually broke, that evening became part of the family folklore, told and retold at many a dinner table, fast food or not.

And in the decades that followed, whenever Margaret passed by any fast-food restaurant, she'd remember that first shared meal—imperfectly perfect, hurried yet so heartwarmingly slow in all the ways that mattered.

20. An Interview with Albert Einstein: The Importance of Curiosity

The sun glistened through the window, casting a soft glow over the vast room filled with endless piles of papers and books. Jerry's footsteps hesitated outside the wooden door. The brass nameplate gleamed, announcing the occupant: "Albert Einstein."

Taking a deep breath, Jerry stepped inside. An overwhelming scent of chalk and paper greeted him. Everywhere he looked, there were scribbles of genius. Amidst this haven of thought sat the man himself, hair unruly, but eyes sharp and welcoming.

"Ah! The young journalist," Einstein exclaimed, pushing aside some papers to make room for Jerry. "You're early. But that's good. Punctuality is the soul of business, after all."

With his heart pounding, Jerry began the interview. He had prepared an exhaustive list of questions—on relativity, quantum mechanics, the very fabric of the universe. But as Einstein began speaking, Jerry found himself enthralled by the physicist's passion and childlike curiosity.

Hours seemed to pass like minutes. At one point, as the evening sun painted the room gold, Einstein paused, lost in thought. "You know," he said, "the most wonderful thing is to be alive and to be curious. The world is a vast, mysterious playground."

The moment was interrupted by the sound of children playing outside. Einstein smiled, "Ah, the real experts on curiosity. Always asking why, why, why."

Jerry chuckled, "I have a daughter, Emily. She's just like that—always exploring, always asking questions."

Einstein's eyes twinkled, "Then she's a scientist at heart. Nurture that. Take her to the stars, dive deep into the mysteries of the ocean, let her feel the wonders of this universe."

A decade later, on cool Saturday mornings, one could find Jerry and young Emily at their local observatory, gazing at the stars. Or sometimes at the museum, marveling at dinosaur bones, or at the park, observing the tiny universe of ants and beetles.

One particular evening, as they lay on their backyard lawn, eyes fixed at the constellation-lit sky, Emily whispered, "Dad, remember when you told me about your interview with Mr. Einstein?"

Jerry smiled, "How can I forget?"

"I think I understand what he meant about the universe being a playground," Emily said, tracing the path of a shooting star.

And there, beneath the vast cosmos, Jerry and Emily shared a silent, beautiful moment. The universe felt close, personal, almost within reach—a canvas of dreams and endless questions, just waiting to be explored.

No profound declarations were made, no grand conclusions drawn. But in the quiet bond of a father and daughter, the spirit of Einstein's words lived on.

Venturing into the Vibrant 1960's

21. The Beatles' Debut on Ed Sullivan

"Come on, Jenny, you're going to miss it!" yelled Sarah, her face illuminated by the glow of the television. The room was abuzz with excitement, a palpable sense of being on the cusp of something monumental.

Jenny dashed from the kitchen, a bowl of popcorn in hand, nearly colliding with Mike and Tom, their neighbors and fellow Beatles enthusiasts. The room was dim, the furniture a little worn, but none of that mattered tonight. The air was thick with anticipation.

As Ed Sullivan introduced the band, the camera panned over to the foursome. Paul, John, George, and Ringo—each face young, hopeful, and bursting with energy. And then the unmistakable opening chords of "I Want to Hold Your Hand" filled the room.

Jenny and Sarah screamed, their voices joining the cacophony of fans onscreen. Mike and Tom tried to maintain a facade of coolness but couldn't resist tapping their feet and bobbing their heads in rhythm.

The world outside might have been cold and still, but inside that little living room, everything was alive and moving. The melodies, the harmonies, the sheer vibrancy of The Beatles—it was as if a switch had been flipped, and black and white had transformed into technicolor.

During a particularly spirited rendition of "She Loves You," Jenny grabbed Sarah's hands, and they danced around, laughing and singing at the top of their lungs. Even the usually-reserved Mike joined in, showcasing some surprisingly good dance moves.

As the final notes echoed and The Beatles took their bow, the room erupted in applause. The energy was electric, a mix of elation and disbelief.

Jenny, catching her breath, turned to Sarah. "Can you believe we just witnessed that?!"

Sarah, eyes shining, replied, "I feel like everything's changed. That was... magic. I bet we'll be talking about this for years."

And indeed, they did. Every gathering, every reunion, the story of that night would be retold with the same fervor. Not just about The Beatles, but about that cozy room, the impromptu dance, and the shared joy of experiencing something unforgettable together.

22. The Arrival of Color TV

The Johnson living room was buzzing with excitement. Young Tommy was practically bouncing on the couch, while his older sister, Lucy, clapped her hands in glee. Their mother, Mrs.

Johnson, had a radiant smile that reached her eyes, reflecting the joy she felt at her family's happiness.

For today was the day: the Johnsons were transitioning from their old black and white set to a brand-new color television.

"Remember when we used to imagine what color Gilligan's shirt was on 'Gilligan's Island'?" Lucy reminisced, nudging Tommy.

He grinned, "Or how we used to guess the color of the sky in 'The Flintstones'!"

Mrs. Johnson chuckled, "And your father and I trying to figure out the exact shade of blue in Perry Mason's eyes."

The room echoed with laughter, their shared memories painting vivid images of days gone by.

The doorbell rang, and Tommy sprinted to open it. Two delivery men rolled in a large box, and the room's energy became palpable. The old set, with its dials and antennas, looked almost antiquated next to the sleek new model.

After the installation, the family gathered around, the remote in Mr. Johnson's hand. With a press of a button, the screen flickered to life. The family gasped collectively. It wasn't just a show; it was a cascade of colors. The greens, the blues, the vibrant yellows—it was all so brilliant, so vivid.

They tuned into "The Wonderful World of Disney," and the children's eyes widened as they saw Sleeping Beauty's castle not in shades of gray, but in mesmerizing colors. The fireworks behind the castle sparkled in hues they'd only imagined.

During the commercial break, Mrs. Johnson brought in a bowl of fruit, placing it next to the screen. "Look!" she exclaimed, "The bananas on the screen are the same color as our bananas!" Everyone chuckled, but there was a truth in her words—they were witnessing the world in their living room, just as it was outside.

Weeks turned into months, and the novelty of the color TV remained. Sunday evenings became an even more special family tradition.

The Johnsons would gather with popcorn and homemade lemonade, watching their favorite shows in technicolor. They laughed at Lucille Ball's antics in vivid reds and cheered for their football team in true-to-life greens.

The seasons changed outside, but inside, the Johnsons' world became more colorful than ever. They celebrated birthdays, holidays, and even simple weekends, with the glow of their color TV adding vibrance to every occasion.

Decades later, Lucy, now with kids of her own, often reminisced about that magical day. "When we got our color TV, it wasn't just about the colors on the screen," she'd say, "It was the color it added to our lives, our memories."

It wasn't about technology; it was about moments—vivid, colorful moments that stayed etched in their hearts forever. And as the years went by, those moments became stories, and those stories... timeless treasures.

23. The First Super Bowl

The January chill was no match for the warmth emanating from the Thompsons' home. Inside, a crackling fireplace, a room full of eager faces, and the soft hum of a television set the stage for what would be a historical evening.

"Jackie, come on! It's starting!" called out Mr. Thompson, settled into his favorite armchair. Beside him, a space was reserved for Jack, his teenage son. The boy, with hair as wild as the 60s and a spark in his eyes, darted in from the kitchen, a bowl of chips in hand.

They were about to watch the first-ever Super Bowl, a face-off between the Green Bay Packers and the Kansas City Chiefs. To Mr. Thompson, a lifelong football enthusiast, this was a dream come true. But more importantly, it was an opportunity to share a monumental moment with his son.

As the game kicked off, Jack, ever the inquisitive teen, shot question after question. "Why are they called quarterbacks? Why is that one wearing a different color helmet?"

Each query was met with a patient response from Mr. Thompson. "The quarterback, son, is like the conductor of an orchestra. He directs the play, sees the field, and makes decisions on the go."

Between plays, Mr. Thompson shared stories from his younger days, of how he and his buddies would play tackle football with makeshift goals in their backyard. They'd mimic the greats, dream of being in their shoes, and now, watching this grand event, those memories felt closer than ever.

Jack listened, his eyes not just on the game but on his father. For every touchdown celebrated, there was a tale from yesteryears, and for every fumble on the screen, a life lesson subtly shared.

Half-time came around, and Mrs. Thompson joined the duo with freshly made hot dogs and cold soda. "Look at you two," she remarked, seeing their matching expressions of glee and anticipation. "Like two peas in a pod."

As the Packers took the lead and eventually won the game, the father-son duo cheered, exchanged high-fives, and fell into a comfortable silence, taking in the magnitude of what they had just witnessed.

When the final whistle blew, Jack turned to his father, "Dad, same time, next year?"

Mr. Thompson smiled, ruffling Jack's hair, "You bet."

And so, a tradition began. Long after teams and champions were forgotten, the memory of that first game, the shared laughter, the stories, and the bond between a father and son persisted.

24. A Day at the Beach Boys Concert

It had been years since Anna and Lisa had truly connected. Time, distance, and life's complexities had gradually widened the gap between them. But on that sun-drenched afternoon in 1966, all it took was the Beach Boys' harmonious tunes to bridge that distance.

The outdoor concert venue was abuzz with excitement. People swarmed in with their picnic blankets, wide-brimmed hats, and oversized sunglasses.

Anna, with her short bob and Lisa, donning a vibrant headband, looked like they had stepped out of two different worlds. Their awkward hello was drowned by the anticipatory murmurs of the crowd.

As the first chords of "Wouldn't It Be Nice" played, the magic began. Anna and Lisa exchanged a glance. This was their song. It was the anthem of their teen years, when summers meant endless days at the beach, sun-kissed skin, and dreams of endless possibilities.

Anna tapped her foot, and Lisa hummed along. By the time "California Girls" played, the two were swaying side by side, laughing as they mimicked the dance moves of their youth. The songs rolled one after the other, each a capsule of memories, of times when the bond between them was unbreakable.

Amidst the chorus of "Surfin' USA", Lisa leaned in, "Remember when we tried surfing after listening to this? We were so bad!"

Anna chuckled, "You ended up with a mouthful of seawater, and I nearly lost my swimsuit!"

The memories flowed as effortlessly as the Beach Boys' melodies. There was the summer of '62 when they built a sandcastle village, the late-night secrets they whispered under the stars, and the pact they made to always have each other's back. Somewhere between "God Only Knows" and "Good Vibrations," years of distance and unsaid words melted away.

The concert drew to an end, the golden sun dipping into the horizon. But the glow between the sisters was undeniable.

"We've missed so much," Lisa whispered, a tear glistening in her eye.

Anna took her hand, "But we're here now, together, and that's all that matters."

The euphoric tunes of the Beach Boys faded into the background as the sisters walked away from the venue, but their connection was rekindled, stronger than ever. They had found their way back to each other, not just as siblings, but as the best friends they had always been.

25. "The Last Pack"

In a surge of resolve, Billy's mom soaked her last pack of cigarettes under the kitchen sink's faucet. "I'm done, Billy. No more!" She declared, while Billy watched, both proud and slightly anxious, recalling stories from school about nicotine withdrawal.

Not an hour later, however, the resolve crumbled. Billy's mom paced the kitchen, clearly fighting an intense craving. Finally, with a sigh, she handed Billy some money and a scribbled note. "Run down to the bar and get me a pack, will you?"

Excitement bubbled within Billy. This felt like a grown-up errand

Billy had never been inside the local bar. It was a place of adult secrets, with a thick aroma of spilled ale and years of stories soaked into its wooden counters.

On any other day, the soft hum of chatter and the clinking of glasses would be drowned out by the bustling town outside. But today, for young Billy, it felt like stepping onto a stage.

Tucking the note and money into a tight fist, he took a hesitant step inside. The room seemed to dim as a few patrons turned their eyes curiously towards the newcomer. He spotted Mr. Jensen from the hardware store and Mrs. Roberts, the librarian, both raising their eyebrows in surprise.

The bartender, a tall man with a gruff face lined with age and experience, looked over. "You lost, kid?" he asked, wiping a glass clean.

Billy, summoning all his courage, approached the counter. "M-mom sent me," he stammered, handing over the note and money. "She needs a pack of her usuals."

The bartender unfolded the note, his eyes scanning it briefly. The humming of the bar seemed to pause. "I've never sold these to you before. This really from your mom?"

Billy nodded, feeling small. "She really needs them. She tried quitting today, but..."

Mr. Jensen chuckled, taking a sip from his glass. "Oh, I remember when I tried quitting. Lasted all of three hours."

But the bartender's face remained serious. "Sorry, kid. I've got rules. Can't just hand these out without being sure."

Billy felt a sinking feeling, imagining going back home empty-handed. He turned to leave, but Mrs. Roberts called out, "Now, now, give the boy a chance. I know his mom and her brand. She's a regular here."

The bartender sighed, torn. "I appreciate that, ma'am, but I have to be sure."

Billy returned home, cheeks burning with embarrassment. "He didn't believe me, Ma," he admitted, bracing for a storm.

Instead, his mom chuckled. "Well, I suppose we'll just have to go and set him straight."

Their joint appearance at the bar made for quite the scene, with laughter and gentle teasing from the regulars. The bartender, sheepishly handing over the cigarettes, apologized, "Just making sure, ma'am. We have to look out for the little ones."

She waved it off, a playful scolding in her eyes. "Always better safe than sorry, right?"

Back home, cigarettes in hand, the duo collapsed into fits of laughter, recounting the day's unexpected escapade. Between giggles, Billy's mom mused, "Maybe it's the universe's way of telling me to truly quit." She winked, "But, for today, one step at a time."

And as the sun set, casting a warm glow into their living room, the two relished in the day's events — a tale of trust, habits, and the whimsical turns life sometimes takes.

26. An Evening at the Drive-In

As the sun slowly retreated, casting a golden hue over the horizon, Lucy and James pulled their car into a spot at the Maple Leaf Drive-In. The theater, which had seen the joyous reactions of countless moviegoers over the years, buzzed with palpable excitement.

Lucy, in her polka-dotted dress, leaned over to James. "I can't believe it's my first time at a drive-in. The stars above, a film ahead—it feels magical," she whispered, her eyes shimmering under the emerging night sky.

James chuckled, a teasing edge in his voice. "Well, considering how much you talk during regular movies, this was the only option left!" They both burst into laughter, the kind that echoed the easy comfort of two souls aligned in happiness.

Inside the car, the dashboard was adorned with a tray of popcorn, soda bottles fizzing from the recent pop, and a tiny radio that would play the film's audio. As twilight deepened, the huge white screen ahead began to brighten with the projector's glow.

Their fingers brushed against each other's as they reached for the popcorn at the same time. It was these little moments, unintended and utterly perfect, that made their bond special.

In the surrounding vehicles, families huddled together under blankets, young kids perched on the car roofs, and couples just like Lucy and James shared whispered dreams and laughter.

When the film began, Lucy's entranced gaze moved from the screen to the stars overhead. The vast expanse of the night sky mirrored the enormity of her feelings—a universe of emotions, with James at the heart of it.

During an intermission, kids ran about with glowing toys while a nearby car played music, leading a few couples to start an impromptu dance. Without hesitation, James pulled Lucy out of the car. They danced, not caring about the steps but moving to their shared rhythm. Around them, the world blurred, and it felt like it was just the two of them, swaying under the canopy of stars.

The second half of the film began, and the two settled back into their seats. They shared a blanket, James' arm comfortably around Lucy. As the movie's climax approached, Lucy rested her head on James' shoulder. Their heartbeats, though silent, seemed to be in sync, echoing the drama playing out on the screen.

As the credits rolled and cars began to depart, James turned to Lucy. "So, how was your first drive-in experience?"

Lucy, her eyes glistening with emotion, simply leaned in and gave him a gentle kiss. Words weren't needed. That simple gesture conveyed the magic of the night and the depth of their feelings.

Driving back home, the world outside felt different—as if the magic of the drive-in had added a layer of enchantment to everything around them.

They knew it wasn't just about the movie; it was about the memories created, the feelings shared, and an evening that would forever remain etched in their hearts.

27. Seeing Mary Poppins

The line at the Regal Theatre stretched around the corner. But for the Thompson family, the excitement overpowered the wait. The marquee above flashed brightly: "Now Showing – Mary Poppins."

It was the kids' first time seeing a movie in a theatre, and the adults were equally abuzz with anticipation.

As they entered, the grandeur of the theatre struck them all—velvet seats, ornate designs on the walls, and a giant screen that promised an escape from reality. The lights dimmed, and as the first notes of the overture wafted through the air, a hush fell over the audience.

Sarah, with her pigtails, sat wide-eyed, clutching her stuffed teddy. Next to her, big brother Jake tried to play it cool, but the twitch of his lips betrayed his excitement. Mom and Dad, Helen and Robert, held hands, both of them transported back to their childhoods, recalling the wonders of their first cinematic experiences.

When Mary Poppins, with her umbrella and carpet bag, appeared on screen, Sarah's gasp echoed a collective feeling of awe. Jake, too cool to gasp, was nonetheless entranced, his foot unconsciously tapping to the rhythm of "A Spoonful of Sugar."

By the time the characters danced with animated penguins, Helen felt a tear trickle down her cheek—not from sadness, but from sheer joy. She looked over at Robert, who was grinning ear to ear, his earlier stress from work now replaced with childlike wonder.

During "Supercalifragilisticexpialidocious," Jake and Sarah whispered attempts to spell the word, giggling at their wild mispronunciations. Every song, every scene seemed to envelop the Thompson family in a world where anything was possible.

Intermission saw the family animatedly discussing their favorite parts so far. Sarah twirled, pretending her teddy was her dance partner, while Jake attempted to use his snack straw as a magical instrument.

Helen and Robert, meanwhile, swapped stories of their movie memories, realizing this outing was as magical for them as it was for the kids.

As the film concluded with Mary Poppins flying away, leaving behind a changed family, the Thompsons felt a change too. The world outside the theater might not have dancing chimney sweeps or laughing tea parties on the ceiling, but it held its magic. The real trick was just to recognize it.

Emerging from the theater, the city lights seemed brighter, the world full of potential adventures. Sarah held her teddy closer, whispering secrets of flying nannies and talking parrots. Jake looked up at the sky, half expecting to see a silhouette with an umbrella.

 And as they walked home, even the streetlamps seemed to hum softly, "Chim chiminey, chim chiminey, chim chim cher-ee…"

28. The Motown Sound

The sun beat down warmly on Elm Street as banners streamed across the lampposts. Smoky aromas from grilling burgers wafted through the air, teasing the taste buds of everyone who passed by. But it wasn't just the tantalizing scent of food that drew people out of their homes—it was the unmistakable, pulsing beat of Motown.

Mrs. Johnson tapped her foot as she set up her lemonade stand. Even the ice cubes seemed to dance in rhythm with the music. The Jones twins, Lila and Lucy, were already twirling in their summer dresses, their giggles synchronizing perfectly with The Temptations' "My Girl."

At the heart of it all was Mr. Anderson's garage. Once a place for tools and old storage boxes, it was now transformed into the neighborhood's own Motown stage. An old record player spun classics, with stacks of vinyl waiting their turn.

The Robinsons, known for their dance-offs, took center stage when "I Can't Help Myself" by the Four Tops came on. Their smooth moves drew cheers and claps.

Soon, a dance circle formed. Little Joey surprised everyone with his moonwalk, while Grandma Rose showed the youngsters she still had groove, reminiscing about seeing Marvin Gaye in her youth.

Mrs. Ramirez shared stories of dancing to Diana Ross and the Supremes during her high school days. She swayed gracefully, her memories painted vividly by the backdrop of the music. Her granddaughter, Mia, watched in awe, realizing that the magic of Motown bridged generations.

As the evening came and the stars began to appear, the soft glow from porch lights illuminated the community. Children, parents, grandparents—all swayed, danced, and sang along.

Stories of first dances, long-lost loves, and summer nights of yesteryears filled the air. And through it all, the beats of Motown continued, like a heart keeping time for Elm Street's collective memories.

When Stevie Wonder's "Isn't She Lovely" started playing, Mr. Thompson took Mrs. Thompson's hand, leading her to the center. Their dance was a gentle, loving testament to years of partnership, making even the teenagers pause and admire.

As the night wound down and the last record spun, the neighborhood sat together, a quilt of ages and stories. The Motown Sound, it seemed, wasn't just music. It was a magical tie, binding them all in shared moments, laughter, and rhythm.

29. The Toy Revolution: Etch A Sketch

Bobby's tenth birthday was extra special because of one iconic red-framed gift: an Etch A Sketch. His eyes widened with excitement as he tore off the wrapping paper. "It's just like the one in the commercials!" he exclaimed.

His sister, Clara, was just as eager to try it out. "Let's draw a house!" she suggested. But as they quickly discovered, the Etch A Sketch was both a delightful and challenging toy. Turning the left knob moved the stylus horizontally, the right one vertically. To draw diagonals, well, that was where the real test lay.

The siblings spent hours on the living room floor, taking turns trying to master it. At first, the results were a series of jagged lines and erratic shapes. Bobby's attempt at a car looked more like a lopsided potato, while Clara's cat eerily resembled a tumbleweed.

Their grandfather chuckled from his armchair. "Let me give it a go," he said, adjusting his glasses. With a twinkle in his eye, he began to turn the knobs with a surprising dexterity. Within minutes, he had etched a recognizable horse. "Learned it at the county fair back in my day," he winked.

Inspired, Bobby and Clara were determined. They practiced diligently, their frustrations turning into little triumphs. The potato-car evolved into a decent-looking vehicle, and the tumbleweed-cat began to resemble a feline.

The Etch A Sketch became a staple in the family home. Guests were greeted with the challenge of drawing something recognizable, leading to many laughs and a few abstract masterpieces. It was more than a toy; it was a conversation starter, an equalizer, a bridge between generations.

Weeks later, Bobby managed to sketch the family home, complete with windows and a chimney emitting curly smoke. Clara drew a sun with rays extending in every direction. Their joy in these accomplishments was palpable, matched only by the pride in their parents' eyes.

Looking back, it wasn't just about the drawings; it was the journey—the challenge, persistence, and the shared moments of joy and frustration.

 The Etch A Sketch was more than a toy; it was a lesson in patience, artistry, and the simple joy of creation. It was a reminder that sometimes, the most treasured memories come from the simplest of pleasures.

30. Disneyland Expands

The Carter family's excitement was palpable as they stepped into the magic of Disneyland. For young Sarah and her older brother Tom, this was not just any ordinary day—it was their first time in this enchanted land. Whispers of new attractions had reached their ears, especially the enchanting "It's a Small World."

Walking down Main Street, Sarah clutched her map, determined to find the newest attractions. The tantalizing aromas of freshly popped popcorn and candy apples filled the air. Every so often, she'd stop, watching in awe as familiar characters from her bedtime stories came to life, parading before her.

"There it is!" Tom exclaimed, pointing towards a whimsical facade with a tower clock that seemed alive with colors and movements. The "It's a Small World" attraction beckoned. The family eagerly queued, the line moving like a winding river, each bend offering glimpses of what awaited inside.

As their boat embarked on its journey, they were serenaded by countless dolls, each singing and dancing to the memorable tune of "It's a Small World." Sarah's eyes widened as the boat glided from one continent to another.

The intricate details of each scene were breathtaking—snow-capped mountains, bustling Asian markets, and European town squares filled with jubilant, dancing dolls.

Grandpa Carter, with his signature cap, leaned down and whispered to Sarah about his time in Europe during the war and how this light-hearted portrayal brought a fresh perspective. Grandma, in turn, chuckled watching the hula dancers, reminding her of her honeymoon in Hawaii.

Exiting the ride, the family found themselves amidst a bustling New Orleans Square. The rhythmic beats of jazz invited them in. They danced, laughed, and even tried some beignets, powdered sugar leaving its trace on their faces.

Later, Tom pulled them towards Adventureland, determined to conquer the Jungle Cruise. The family laughed at the skipper's pun-filled commentary, spotting hippos and marveling at the backside of water.

As the sun began to set, casting a golden hue over Sleeping Beauty's Castle, they found a spot for the parade. The illuminated floats, characters dancing, and music brought together the day's adventures into one harmonious finale.

With fireworks painting the night sky, the Carters stood, hand in hand. Disneyland had not just offered them rides; it had provided stories, bridged generational gaps, and gifted them memories that would be cherished for a lifetime.

31. The Bond Phenomenon

In the dim light of the living room, young Timmy twirled an imaginary pistol, trying to mimic the iconic pose of James Bond. Every so often, he'd glance at his dad, hoping for approval.

Mr. Thompson, with a twinkle in his eye, played along, adjusting Timmy's stance ever so slightly. Their excitement was palpable—they were heading to the cinema to catch the latest Bond flick.

As they stepped into the theater, the familiar scent of buttered popcorn wafted towards them. Timmy, wide-eyed, noticed the poster of Bond, complete with his sharp tuxedo and signature smirk. He felt a rush of adrenaline; this wasn't just any movie—it was an adventure.

The lights dimmed, the classic theme song began, and the world of espionage unfolded before them.

Every car chase had Timmy gripping the armrest, every clever quip between Bond and the villains had him and his father chuckling, and the exotic locations made them dream of faraway places.

During a tense scene, Mr. Thompson leaned over, whispering to Timmy about the Cold War and the real spies that inspired such tales. History mingled seamlessly with the silver screen, and Bond's escapades became more than just entertainment.

After the credits rolled, they stepped out into the bright afternoon, with Timmy already reenacting his favorite scenes. But more than the action, it was the bond (pun intended) between father and son that had strengthened.

Their shared excitement, the whispered historical asides, and the dreamy plans of visiting those far-off places together made the day unforgettable.

For years to come, the adventures of 007 became their little tradition—a way for two generations to connect over the magic of cinema and the tales of a bygone era.

32. Classic Family TV Shows

The living room hummed with anticipation. The family's old television set, with its chunky buttons and dials, was switched on a bit earlier than usual. Tonight was the premiere of "The Andy Griffith Show", and they'd been waiting for this all week.

Mom's apple pie rested on the coffee table, steam wafting up. Dad fiddled with the rabbit ears to get a clearer picture, and just as he succeeded, the first familiar whistles of the show's theme song filled the room.

Eyes fixed on the screen, they entered Mayberry, laughing at Barney's goof-ups, shaking their heads at Opie's antics. The room echoed with chuckles and shared glances - those fleeting moments when a scene or a line resonated.

During commercials, Grandma reminisced about her hometown while Lucy kept trying to mimic Barney's walk, causing bursts of laughter.

As the credits began to roll, Lucy broke the brief silence. "Can we get some ice cream at Floyd's Barbershop?" Everyone chuckled.

The TV screen went blank, but no one moved immediately. The room was filled with the residual joy of shared experience. Dad got up to turn off the set, and the soft light from the living room lamp painted the room in a warm glow.

There was a simple delight in watching a show together, feeling the characters come to life in your own living room. But it wasn't just about the show, it was the shared glances, the in-between moments, the playful banter.

Lucy, pie crumbs on her lips, snuggled into her blanket. The sound of soft chatter in the background and the taste of sweet pie were now forever linked to the comforting world of Mayberry.

33. The Surfing Craze

Golden sun rays danced over the waves, which lapped the

shores of California's sandy beaches. In the distance, the rhythmic melodies of The Beach Boys wafted in the air, blending with the scent of saltwater and sunscreen.

Among the beachgoers were four friends: Mark, Elsie, Bobby, and Jane. Driven by the tales of the emerging surfing culture, they decided to embrace the wave-riding challenge headfirst. Or in Bobby's case, quite literally.

Their first attempts were a mixture of playful tumbles and saltwater-filled noses. Mark had a knack for balance, but Elsie was all enthusiasm with very little coordination.

Jane, ever the academic, had read three books on surfing and was busy offering theoretical advice, while Bobby's wild antics had more than one onlooker stifling a laugh.

One sunny afternoon, an older surfer named Diego approached the group. With sun-bleached hair and a deeply tanned complexion, he had seen more waves than they could ever dream of. "You youngsters remind me of my crew back in the day," he said with a grin, offering to give them a few pointers.

Under Diego's guidance, the ocean's once intimidating waves became playgrounds of potential. Each friend progressed in their own way. Mark's graceful turns drew appreciative nods, while Elsie's once flailing attempts had now become determined rides towards the beach.

Jane's theoretical knowledge blended with her growing practical experience, and she soon carved the waves with precision. And Bobby? Well, he still had his wipeouts, but he was undeterred, always surfacing with a big grin.

The days turned into weeks, and the coastline became their second home. Beach bonfires, impromptu guitar jams, and stories shared under the tapestry of stars became commonplace.

The surfing craze wasn't just about catching the best wave; it was about the friends you made along the way and the shared memories etched against the backdrop of the vast ocean.

One day, after a particularly exhilarating session, the friends lay sprawled on their beach towels, exhausted but content. The setting sun painted the horizon in hues of pink and gold.

As the familiar strains of "Surfin' USA" drifted from a nearby radio, Mark spoke up, "You know, I think we've found our little slice of the California dream."

Elsie, looking at the shimmering water, replied, "It was never about being the best surfer. It was about the sun, the sea, and this." She gestured to the close-knit circle they formed.

Each of them knew, in that fleeting moment that the waves might come and go, but their bond, fortified by shared spills and thrills, was here to stay.

34. An Afternoon with Dr. Seuss

A whirlwind of excitement rushed through Pinegrove Elementary when Mrs. Simmons, the soft-spoken librarian, announced a special visitor: none other than Dr. Seuss himself! The classrooms were abuzz, but in the back, little Timmy just shrugged. Books had never been his strong suit.

On the day, children gathered in the school hall, their tiny shoes clicking and clacking. The stage had a singular chair, a table, and atop it, Dr. Seuss's iconic hat. But where was the man himself?

Suddenly, from behind a curtain, out stepped a tall figure, whiskers prominent and smile wide. It was him! Dr. Seuss, with a playful twinkle in his eye, began to recite, and the magic of his tales enveloped the room. From Whoville to the Lorax, every story danced and sang.

Yet, it was when he began "Oh, the Places You'll Go!" that Timmy, previously uninterested, leaned forward. The rhythm, the promise of adventures and dreams, struck a chord in his young heart. Here was a world in words he had never imagined.

After the session, as children clamored for autographs, Timmy approached with a different request. "Can I read more stories like yours?" Dr. Seuss, delighted, handed him a signed book and whispered, "Remember, young man, to find the magic between the pages."

Years flew by, and Timmy's love for reading grew. That singular afternoon had not only ignited a passion for books but also a desire to share their wonders.

He went on to become Mr. Timothy, the favorite teacher at Pinegrove Elementary, often seen with a familiar hat and a Seussian book, ready to introduce another young mind to the magic that once transformed his world.

35. Instant Photography

The Martins were buzzing with excitement, having just packed their station wagon for their annual summer road trip. This year, though, they had a new family member: the Polaroid camera. No more waiting weeks to see their vacation snaps—now, they'd have their memories in a matter of moments.
As the car rumbled on, scenic vistas rolling by, young Lucy, camera in hand, was keen to document it all. "Stop the car!" she'd yell, spying a picturesque field of sunflowers or an old, rustic barn. And with each scenic spot, out would pop the iconic square photo.

At their campsite, little Joey's marshmallow-on-fire fiasco was immortalized forever, his wide eyes and open mouth causing a round of giggles every time the photo was passed around the campfire that night.

When Aunt Marge tried to teach the kids to fish and ended up falling into the stream? Well, that wet, surprised expression was now a family classic.

Perhaps the most special moment, though, came at sunset on the beach. The entire family, including the ever-reluctant teenager Jake, gathered together, the pastel sky painting a perfect backdrop.

Lucy set the timer, and the camera clicked. In the still of the evening, they watched in awe as the image slowly revealed itself: the Martins, in all their joy and silliness, framed by nature's splendor.

By the end of the vacation, their photo album was plump with instant memories. And as they unpacked back home, the Polaroid photos weren't just images—they were moments of time, immediately lived and immediately cherished.

Many summers came and went, but that year, with the magic of instant photography, remained especially vivid.

Even decades later, Lucy would often find herself looking at that sunset beach photo, feeling the sand between her toes and hearing the gentle rush of waves, a smile growing as she remembered the summer the Martins held time in their hands.

36. The Sweetness of Candy Land

The rain outside tapped gently against the window, the gloomy weather threatening to dampen the spirits of young Emma and Max, who were visiting their grandparents for the weekend. But in the cozy living room, there was no hint of gloom, only excitement, as Grandma pulled out a colorful box from the old wooden cupboard.

"Your mother and I used to play this on rainy days like this," she said, revealing the Candy Land board with its winding path of bright squares, surrounded by fantastical candy constructions. Grandpa chuckled as he set up another board, "And here's Chutes and Ladders for when you're done with the candy world!"

Max's eyes widened, "Wow! They look so fun! But... how do you swipe or tap on them?" Grandpa laughed heartily, "No swiping here, these games are all about imagination and luck!"

As the children picked their characters, Emma chose the iconic Princess Lolly while Max opted for Mr. Mint. They were immediately enchanted. The game was simple, yet every draw of a colored card that dictated their journey brought squeals of delight or mock expressions of dismay.

There were triumphant moments when Emma sprinted ahead, landing on a rainbow trail, and groans when Max found himself sliding down a chute, only to start climbing a ladder again with renewed vigor.

Grandpa, on the other hand, was teaching patience and the twists of fate with Chutes and Ladders. "Life's a bit like this game," he mused. "Sometimes you climb, sometimes you fall, but you keep moving."

Hours seemed to fly by. The rain outside became a distant memory, replaced by the rich tales Grandma and Grandpa shared of their game nights as children. The room echoed with laughter, playful banter, and the rustle of cards and spinners.

When the evening drew to a close, Emma and Max, clutching their new favorite board games, shared a secret look. No video game had ever given them this kind of joy. It was the joy of shared moments, of stories told and retold, of simple games that bound generations.

Outside, the rain had stopped, but inside, the warmth lingered, a sweetness that went beyond any candy or game, a sweetness of shared memories and timeless love.

37. Julia Child and the Joy of Cooking

Linda and Richard had fallen into a routine. After years of marriage, take-out meals and microwaved dinners seemed easier than cooking from scratch. But one evening, as they flicked through TV channels, they stumbled upon a charismatic woman with a distinctive voice, teaching the art of French cooking.

It was none other than Julia Child, with her endearing mix of elegance and clumsiness. She wasn't just cooking; she was creating magic with butter, flour, and a sprinkle of humor. The couple was instantly captivated.

Inspired, Linda rummaged through the back of their kitchen cabinet and dusted off a neglected cookbook. "How about we try making that boeuf bourguignon Julia was talking about?" she mused, looking at Richard with a twinkle in her eye.

Richard, ever the adventurous spirit, chuckled, "Only if you promise to do the Julia voice!" That evening, their kitchen came alive in a way it hadn't for years. There was laughter, a few mishaps with flour dusting the counters like snow, and even an impromptu dance with a wooden spoon as a microphone.

Following Julia's guidance from the television, they marveled at how she made complex dishes seem achievable. Her joy was infectious, her passion evident. And though their rendition of boeuf bourguignon wasn't perfect, it was made with heaps of love.

The next week, they tackled coq au vin. Then came the chocolate mousse. Their dining table, once a mere place to eat, transformed into a canvas of colors, tastes, and shared memories. Friends and family began to join, lured by the delightful aromas wafting from their kitchen.

Years later, their granddaughter would say, "I think Grandma and Grandpa fell in love all over again because of that lady on TV with the funny voice."

She wasn't wrong. Julia Child, with her boundless enthusiasm, hadn't just taught them recipes. She had served them a reminder of the joy in shared endeavors and the magic that bubbles away in a pot when two hearts cook together.

38. The Space Race and Model Rockets

July 20, 1969. The faint blue glow from the television set lit up Tommy's awestruck face. Neil Armstrong's boots pressed into the moon's dusty surface, and households around the world leaned in to watch.

In the midst of the living room clutter, 10-year-old Tommy clutched a toy rocket, imagining it floating beside the real Apollo 11. "Dad," he whispered, "Can we build one?"

The very next weekend, Tommy's backyard buzzed with activity. They didn't have NASA's budget, but what they lacked in funds, they made up for in enthusiasm. There were sketches, cardboard tubes, a mess of glue, and an impatient boy waiting for the paint to dry.

The first launch was an intimate affair. Just Tommy, his dad, and a few starry-eyed neighborhood kids. "3... 2... 1..." they chanted. With a fizz and puff of smoke, their tiny rocket soared – not quite reaching the moon, but certainly touching the clouds.

Subsequent weekends followed the same ritual. With each launch, Tommy's rockets grew more intricate, each one bearing the hopes of reaching just a bit higher than the last. The 'moon landings' were celebrated with ice cream and laughter, regardless of the rocket's actual height.

One summer afternoon, as another rocket made its descent, Tommy didn't rush to retrieve it. Instead, he lay on the grass, looking up, lost in thought. His dad joined him, their heads almost touching, both ensnared by the vastness of the sky.

No words were exchanged, just the ambient noise of cicadas and the distant laughter of children. Two generations, side by side, each with dreams as vast and boundless as the universe itself.

39. The Merry-Go-Round of Music: Jukeboxes

Daisy's Diner was more than just a place to grab a bite. With its checkered floors and neon lights, it was a portal to another era. The centerpiece, gleaming under the soft lights, was the jukebox: a treasure trove of melodies and memories.

Every Saturday night, Sarah, Jack, Clara, and Leo would slide into their favorite red booth, a handful of coins ready for the musical journey they'd embark on. The excitement was palpable as they took turns selecting a track. The pressing of buttons, followed by the jukebox whirring to life, held a magic of its own.

When the notes of "Can't Help Falling in Love" started, Clara's eyes glistened. "Our prom song," she whispered to Jack, recalling the timid steps and nervous laughter. They exchanged glances, holding hands beneath the table.
Sarah chuckled, slipping another coin, and choosing "Twist and Shout." Instantly, the diner came alive, as memories of carefree dance-offs took over. Leo, with a twinkle in his eyes, reminisced, "Remember trying to recreate those dance moves at my backyard party? We were quite the performers!"

One by one, each song became more than just notes and lyrics; they were fragments of shared pasts, stitched together by laughter, tears, and youthful adventures.

As the night deepened, the friends grew quiet, lost in their individual reveries, punctuated only by the sounds of their favorite hits. Each song transported them back to a moment, some bittersweet, others joyfully ridiculous, but all unforgettable.

Finally, as the last coin was spent and "What a Wonderful World" filled the room, the four friends shared a moment of silence. It was Sarah who broke it, "Every time we're here, it feels like time stops, even if just for a moment."

With contented sighs, they left the diner, the soft glow of the jukebox fading behind them. The melodies remained, however, etched forever in their hearts, a testament to shared moments and timeless friendships.

40. A Dance with Jackie Kennedy

The soft amber lights of the grand ballroom shimmered, casting a golden hue over everyone. Serviceman Richard's heart raced with a mix of excitement and nervousness. Invitations to such events were rare for someone of his rank, and yet here he was, at one of Washington's grandest affairs.

The music wafted from a live band, a sultry jazz that made couples glide on the dance floor. Richard, although decent in his dance moves, felt like an outlier, in awe of the glittering crowd.

As he sipped his drink, trying to find familiar faces, there she was. Jacqueline Kennedy, the First Lady herself, a picture of elegance and grace. Richard's heart missed a beat. He had seen her in newspapers and on the black-and-white TV screen, but in person, her charm was unparalleled.

As the evening wore on, an old tune began to play. Suddenly, there was a soft tap on his shoulder. He turned around to find the First Lady, her eyes twinkling mischievously.

"Care to dance, serviceman?" she asked.

Gobsmacked, Richard could only nod, praying his feet wouldn't betray him.

 As they moved, her poise made it feel like they were floating. Their chat was easy and unhurried, her humility shining through as they spoke of everyday things: the joy of a good book, the taste of ice cream on a summer day, and the sound of children's laughter.

As the song ended, she whispered, "Thank you for the dance," and with a smile, she moved on, leaving Richard momentarily stunned.

As he rejoined his comrades, he found himself humming the tune they had danced to, each note imprinted with the memory of that enchanting evening.

His buddies, noticing his gleeful spirit, nudged him with curious eyes, but all Richard could do was smile, knowing that some moments are too precious to be put into words.

Journey to the Jivin' 1970's

41. An Audience with Pope John Paul II

Lena's heart was heavy as she walked the cobbled streets of Rome, the weight of recent heartbreak and loss pressing down on her.

She had always dreamt of visiting this city, but never imagined it would be under these circumstances. As she roamed the city's ancient corridors, she stumbled upon a flyer: "Mass led by Pope John Paul II at St. Peter's Square." On a whim, she decided to attend.

The morning of the Mass was unusually cool, with a soft, golden sunlight piercing through the iconic dome of St. Peter's Basilica. As Lena sat amidst the sea of faces, the air thick with anticipation, she felt a kinship, an unspoken bond with strangers from around the world.

When Pope John Paul II emerged, the crowd fell into a hushed reverence. His presence was magnetic, his voice, though soft, echoed with warmth and conviction.

As he spoke, Lena felt the weight of her sorrows lift, even if just a little. His words weren't just religious; they spoke of resilience, hope, and the shared human experience.

A particular moment captured Lena's heart. A young child, no older than six, somehow broke free from the crowd and ran towards the Pope. Instead of being stopped, the child was lifted by the Pope into his arms. They exchanged a few whispered words, their exchange unseen but deeply felt by everyone. The child's innocent laughter and the Pope's gentle embrace became a symbol of universal love and care.

After the Mass, Lena felt a newfound peace. It wasn't just the words or the rituals, but the collective faith and shared moments of tenderness that warmed her heart.

Years later, when recounting her time in Rome, Lena wouldn't speak of the tourist spots or the Italian delicacies.

Instead, she would reminisce about that morning in St. Peter's Square, and how, in her loneliest moment, she found solace in a sea of strangers and the kind words of a Pope.

42. The Rise of Home Video

The Thompson living room was buzzing with excitement. It was the first Saturday since they'd brought home the shiny new VHS player, a gadget that looked somewhat out of place on their old wooden TV stand. Mrs. Thompson had just returned from the video store, her arms laden with a selection of films for their inaugural family movie night.

"Lights, camera, action!" declared Mr. Thompson, his voice filled with mock gravity, making the kids giggle. With a dramatic flourish, he pushed the bulky cassette into the player. There was a soft whirring sound, then magic. Their once ordinary living room was transformed into a private cinema.

Young Jenny, with her golden curls, was snuggled between her parents, her eyes wide in wonder. Beside them, teenage Jake tried to act nonchalant, pretending he wasn't as excited as his little sister, though his intense gaze betrayed him.

The films were a delightful mix of comedy, drama, and adventure. The family laughed, cheered, and sometimes even shed a tear or two. The room was filled with the scent of buttered popcorn, the soft glow of the TV screen, and the shared warmth of being together.

During an intermission, Jake shared his own amateur film, a funny skit he and his friends had recorded at school. The Thompsons laughed till their sides hurt, watching their son's antics and the joy he found with his friends.

As the final credits rolled, Jenny, yawning, asked if they could do this every Saturday. Mrs. Thompson smiled, replying, "We'll see." Jake just grinned, already planning the next video to rent.

The VHS player, with its quirky rewind noise and temperamental pause button, became a centerpiece in the Thompson living room. Every Saturday, the family would gather around it, each movie night a new chapter in their shared story.

43. The Pet Rock Phenomenon

Mrs. Henderson, a spry 78-year-old, lived alone in her small apartment since her beloved cat Whiskers passed away. Her days were quiet, and she missed the companionship, but she had resigned herself to her solitude. That was until her cheeky granddaughter, Lily, visited one day, presenting her with a peculiar gift—a Pet Rock.

"His name's Rocky," Lily explained, trying to stifle her giggles. "I thought you might need some company. And he's very low-maintenance!"

Mrs. Henderson squinted at the smooth, ordinary-looking rock. "Well, isn't he... interesting?" she remarked, genuinely puzzled.

Deciding to play along, she placed Rocky on her windowsill. Every morning, she'd greet him with a cheerful, "Good morning, Rocky!" before watering her plants. At night, she'd bid him goodnight, his quiet presence oddly comforting.

As days turned into weeks, Mrs. Henderson found herself talking to Rocky more and more. She told him stories of her youth, her adventures, and of course, about Whiskers. She'd chuckle, imagining what the rock would say if it could speak.

One evening, her neighbor Mrs. Palmer visited, curious about Mrs. Henderson's newfound joy. As they sipped their tea, Mrs. Henderson introduced Rocky, recounting the tale of his arrival. The women laughed heartily, sharing memories of other fads and crazes they had witnessed.

Word spread about Mrs. Henderson's quirky new friend. Neighbors, young and old, popped in, each wanting a glimpse of the famous Rocky. Many brought their own Pet Rocks, and soon, impromptu 'Pet Rock Parties' became a neighborhood sensation.

Rocky, the silent stone, had done something remarkable. He not only brought a smile to Mrs. Henderson's face but also revived a community spirit that had been dormant.

One sunny afternoon, as Mrs. Henderson dusted her living room, she paused and looked at Rocky, now surrounded by several other rock buddies on the sill. With a twinkle in her eye, she whispered, "Thank you, Rocky. Who knew such a tiny rock could make such a big ripple!"

44. Billy Graham's Revival Meeting

Amidst the clamor and hustle of the 60s, the Morrisons, like many families, found themselves drifting apart, ensnared by the era's challenges. Sunday church visits became sporadic, and evening prayers were often forgotten.

When news spread of Billy Graham's crusade coming to town, Mrs. Morrison thought it might be a refreshing change. The children, Anna and Mark, were hesitant. "Do we have to?" they groaned. But Mr. Morrison, sensing an opportunity, insisted, "Just this once, for your mother."

The stadium was packed, a sea of hopeful faces. As the family settled into their seats, the atmosphere was palpable, filled with a mix of anticipation and reverence.

And then Billy Graham stepped up, his voice a balm on the restless souls. His words weren't new or groundbreaking. But the sincerity, the conviction, the passion—it resonated. He spoke of love, of forgiveness, of community. He painted a vivid picture of a life anchored in faith and service.

Anna felt a tear trickle down her cheek, not entirely sure why. Mark, typically restless, sat rapt, hanging onto every word. Mr. and Mrs. Morrison exchanged glances, sensing a shift in their family's axis.

When the evening ended, and they walked back to their car, there was a newfound lightness in their steps, a bond that felt repaired. Anna broke the silence, "Can we volunteer at the community kitchen this weekend?" Mark nodded, "I'd like that."

The Morrisons didn't transform overnight, but the crusade was a catalyst. Sundays saw them at church, not out of obligation but genuine desire. They started hosting neighborhood gatherings, bridging gaps and forging bonds. Service became integral, not incidental.

Years later, as Anna leafed through the family photo album with her grandchildren, they came across a black and white picture of that evening. "What was this, grandma?" the youngest asked.

"That," Anna began, with a nostalgic smile, "was the night we decided to be more than just a family living under the same roof. We chose to be involved, to listen, to support." She paused, her eyes misting up. "We became the Morrisons that evening."

The room was quiet for a moment, the children lost in imagination, picturing the young Anna in a crowded stadium, forever changed by an evening's sermon.

The crackling sound of the fireplace and the soft glow it cast was all that filled the room, as memories of a bygone era came alive once more.

45. The Star Wars Saga Begins

The year was 1977. In a time before social media and spoilers, buzz spread the old-fashioned way—through word of mouth, radio, and newspaper ads. One film was on everyone's lips: Star Wars.

Jerry's excitement was palpable. He had heard fantastical tales about this new space opera and was eager to see it for himself.

In fact, Jerry was so excited that he rallied his family together, ensuring that they'd be among the first in town to see it. His daughter Lucy, with her golden pigtails, was skeptical. "Is it better than our Saturday cartoons?" she asked skeptically.

Holding Lucy's hand, the family joined the swelling line outside the cinema. Parents chatted animatedly, kids played with makeshift lightsabers crafted from rolled-up newspapers, and the atmosphere was electric.

The large, colorful poster outside depicted characters none of them recognized yet—but soon, names like Luke Skywalker, Princess Leia, and Darth Vader would be household staples.

The lights dimmed, and as the iconic opening crawl began, a hush fell over the audience. It was a shared journey into a galaxy far, far away. There were gasps of awe, laughter, and an overwhelming sense of adventure that bridged generations.

Emerging from the theater, Lucy, eyes wide, whispered to Jerry, "That was better than a hundred Saturdays." He chuckled, ruffling her hair, "Told you."

On the way home, Lucy perched by the car window, gazing up at the night sky. She pointed towards the stars and said, "Dad, do you think there's a real galaxy out there like in the movie?"

Jerry smiled, squeezing her hand, "With the universe so vast, who knows? Maybe, just maybe, there's another adventure waiting out there." And as they drove off, the world seemed a little bit bigger and filled with even more wonder.

46. Meeting Fred Rogers

It was a typical Saturday for little Emma—morning cartoons, followed by playing in the yard. However, today was different. Today she was going to the local public television station's fundraiser with her parents. The selling point? Mister Rogers would be there.

Emma could barely contain her excitement. Every day, she eagerly awaited Mister Rogers' gentle voice, singing, "Won't you be my neighbor?" She clutched her red sweater, identical to the one Mister Rogers wore, and she even had her tiny sneakers for the occasion.

As they entered the station, Emma saw the set of Mister Rogers' Neighborhood. The iconic trolley, the castle, and...there he was, Mister Rogers himself. Fred Rogers stood amidst the crowd, radiating warmth and kindness. Emma felt her heart race.

When her turn came, Mister Rogers bent down to her level, his eyes twinkling with genuine interest. "Well, hello there, neighbor," he greeted softly.

Overwhelmed, Emma simply handed him her red sweater. Mister Rogers smiled, understandingly, and said, "It's such a special day when we get to meet our television neighbors in person."

Emma whispered, "I wear this sweater because of you." Mister Rogers' smile deepened. "And every time you wear it, remember to spread kindness, just as you've shown me today."

The day faded, but the memory of that encounter never did. Emma didn't just wear her red sweater more often; she embodied the spirit of Mister Rogers. She helped a new student feel welcome, consoled friends when they were down, and was the first to share her toys.

Years passed, and while the red sweater no longer fit, Emma's heart remained as warm as ever. Every act of kindness she performed, she remembered the gentle man who once told her the power of being a good neighbor.

As she taught her own children the value of compassion, she'd often recount that magical day, proving that sometimes, a single meeting can shape a lifetime.

47. A Taste of Fondue

1975 was a year of flair pants, roller skates, and the hypnotic beats of ABBA. But for Martha and George, it was the year of the fondue.

Having heard the latest craze from their trendy friends, the couple decided to host their very own fondue party. They invested in a brand-new fondue set—a shiny pot surrounded by color-coded forks, promising a night of melted delight and fun.

Invitations were sent, RSVPs received, and excitement brewed. George took charge of mixing the perfect cheese blend, while Martha meticulously cubed bread, prepared vegetables, and, for the brave-hearted, chunks of meat for the broth fondue.

Guests began to trickle in, their interest piqued by the unfamiliar yet inviting aroma. The living room was alive with chatter, the warm glow from the fondue pot casting playful shadows.

As George carefully guided his first guest on the dipping etiquette, a ripple of laughter broke out. Mischievously, Martha shared the folklore—drop your bread, and you'll be kissing the person next to you. Blushes and chuckles ensued.

Soon, the room was filled with stories shared over the pot. Every dip was a mini-adventure, sometimes resulting in a lost morsel, leading to playful jests and exaggerated tales of "fondue rescues."

Amidst the dipping and laughing, a lovely thing happened. Barriers melted away just like the cheese in the pot. The bond between neighbors, friends, and even mere acquaintances grew stronger. Conversations flowed from movies like Jaws to the latest vinyl record someone had purchased.

As the night drew to a close, with bellies full and spirits high, everyone knew they'd been part of something special. A simple culinary experiment had turned into an evening of connection and shared memories.

In the years that followed, many things changed—music, fashion, and even culinary trends.

But every now and then, when Martha and George would bump into an old friend in town, they'd exchange knowing smiles, remembering a night where a pot of melted cheese bridged hearts and stirred shared stories. That fondue set, now a relic in their kitchen, became their quiet testimony to a night when the '70s spirit truly came alive.

48. Family Camping Trips

The sun kissed the horizon, casting a soft orange hue over the vast, untouched landscape. The Sullivan family—Paul, Maggie, and their two kids, Tommy and Lily—stood by their newly pitched tent, taking in the scenic beauty of the natural reserve they'd chosen for their weekend getaway.

Paul, who had grown up listening to stories of family camping trips from his parents and grandparents, wanted to recreate those cherished moments. "No gadgets, no distractions," he'd declared, "Just us and Mother Nature."

The first day was filled with hiking, fishing, and a picnic by the lakeside. Tommy and Lily, used to the bustling city life, stared in wonder at the fluttering butterflies and scampered after playful squirrels, their laughter echoing in the serene surroundings.

As evening approached, they gathered around the campfire. The soft glow illuminated their faces as they roasted marshmallows, making s'mores while the crickets played their nighttime symphony.

Paul pulled out his old guitar, strumming tunes from his youth, while Maggie, with her mellifluous voice, sang along. They introduced their children to classics from their own childhoods, songs filled with tales of love, adventure, and hope.

That night, the family lay outside the tent, gazing up at the star-studded sky. "Look, there's Orion!" Tommy exclaimed. Paul began narrating stories about constellations, just as his grandfather had done for him.

Each star had its own story, and as the tales flowed, the vast expanse of the universe seemed to draw closer, enveloping the family in its mystique.

The next day, a light drizzle greeted them. But instead of dampening their spirits, it only added to the adventure. Donning raincoats, the Sullivans embarked on a treasure hunt.

They trudged through the wet grass, deciphered clues, and laughed heartily at their misadventures. When they finally found the 'treasure'—a box filled with old family photos—it brought tears to Paul and Maggie's eyes. Pictures of their own childhood camping trips, faces of loved ones, and memories of bygone days.

The weekend came to an end all too quickly, but as they packed up, the air was filled with contentment. They had found more than just a break from their routine; they had discovered the ties that bound them as a family.

The car ride back was filled with chatter. Tommy and Lily, with bright eyes, recounted their adventures, already looking forward to the next trip. Maggie held Paul's hand, a silent promise of more such beautiful memories to come.

It wasn't just about escaping the city or being amidst nature; it was about finding themselves and reconnecting. The Sullivan family had uncovered the simple joys of togetherness and the magic that the great outdoors held.

49. Saturday Morning Cartoons

The first rays of the sun peeked through the curtains, casting a soft glow on the room. Two sets of eyes popped open almost simultaneously. It was the most awaited time of the week for the Bennett siblings, Timmy and Lila. Saturday. The day of cartoons!

Clad in their favorite pajamas—Timmy's with Scooby-Doo and Lila's adorned with the Pink Panther—they tiptoed past their parents' room and made a beeline for the living room. The television flickered to life, the colorful graphics and cheerful music filling the air.

It was their ritual. A giant bowl of cereal in their laps, the two would lose themselves in the adventures of Mystery Inc. and the hilarious antics of the Pink Panther.

 The villains in Scooby-Doo were always "meddling kids" away from success, and no matter how many times they watched,

Timmy and Lila would laugh, cheer, and even shout out advice to the screen.

The commercials, too, were a part of the charm. Singing jingles of the newest toys or cereals, they became mini-experts, exchanging reviews during the cartoon breaks. "I bet the 'Super Looper Plane' isn't as fun as it looks," Timmy would declare, while Lila would dreamily talk about the newest dollhouse she'd seen.

The day unfolded with animated mysteries and laugh-out-loud capers, each episode a tapestry of joy for the young minds. And as the final notes of their favorite shows echoed in the room, the real magic began.

With animated excitement, Timmy and Lila would scramble to find paper and crayons, drawing out their own versions of the morning's stories. Sometimes, they'd even enact little plays, with Lila giving her best Daphne impression and Timmy trying to outdo her with his Pink Panther antics.

Their grandmother, always their most enthusiastic audience, would clap and laugh, sometimes joining in with a character role of her own.

It was these moments, after the shows ended, that the true spirit of those Saturday mornings came alive. It wasn't just about watching; it was about creating, imagining, and bonding over shared stories.

As the clock's hands moved towards afternoon, the television would be turned off, but the echoes of laughter and the remnants of drawn adventures lay scattered around, testament to another morning well spent.

For the Bennett kids, Saturdays were more than just cartoons; they were a gateway to a world of imagination, where anything was possible, and every story was just a beginning.

50. Jaws: The Thrill of the Theater

The golden hour cast long shadows as Mark, Jenny, and their tight-knit group of friends eagerly made their way to the grand old cinema in the heart of town. The film "Jaws" was making waves, no pun intended, with everyone talking about the terrifying shark that lurked in its scenes. This was the film event of the year, and no one wanted to be left out.

The theater, with its vintage marquee lights, painted a nostalgic picture, reminiscent of days when cinema outings were the highlight of one's week. Friends and strangers alike lined up, their chatter contributing to an atmosphere thick with anticipation. While in line, they swapped stories of beach adventures, playfully exaggerating shark tales, all in good fun and in the spirit of the evening.

Once inside, they were greeted by the scent of buttery popcorn and the soft velvety touch of the theater seats. The hall was packed, every seat filled with someone eager to be thrilled. As the lights slowly faded, a communal silence took over.

The film delivered on every account. Shared gasps, collective jumps, and communal laughter painted a picture more vivid than any scene. Mark found himself both covering Jenny's eyes during tense moments and being reassured by her during others.

Towards the climax, the entire theater seemed to share a heartbeat, pounding in rhythm to the suspenseful background score. And when it ended, instead of an immediate burst of conversation, there was a beautiful, shared silence. A moment of reflection.

Emerging into the cool night air, the group felt bonded in a way that only shared experiences can foster. As they made their way to a nearby diner, they animatedly discussed every twist and turn, every jump and scare.

At the diner, over late-night snacks, they made a pact. Every year, they would gather to watch a film together, reliving the magic of shared cinematic experiences. However, as they reminisced about the movie that night, Mark posed a question, "What was the real takeaway from 'Jaws'?"

Jenny, taking a moment to think, replied, "It's not just about the shark or the suspense. It's about facing our fears, coming together, and finding strength in unity."

The table nodded in agreement. And it was then that they decided to not just watch movies together but to face life's challenges head-on, as a united front.

Whenever one faced a 'shark' in their life, be it a challenge or fear, they knew they could rely on this group for support. Because the real thrill wasn't just in watching a movie together; it was in navigating the unpredictable waters of life with trusted friends by your side.

51. ABBA Mania

Flares, glittering costumes, and the distinct beat of 'Dancing Queen' echoing from the massive speakers - the stadium was alive with the electric energy of ABBA fans. In the midst of this euphoria were Sophie, Maria, Alex, and Jake, a close-knit group of friends who had grown up with ABBA's tunes as the soundtrack to their most cherished memories.

Sophie twirled her long, feathered boa, laughing as Maria tried to mimic the iconic dance steps they'd seen on their TV screens countless times.

Alex, always the shy one, suddenly found his groove, moving to the music with a freedom that surprised even himself. Jake, wearing oversized sunglasses, captured every moment on his instant camera, knowing these were memories they would treasure forever.

As the opening notes of 'Mamma Mia' played, the entire stadium seemed to unite, singing in joyous harmony. The friends held onto each other, swaying, and singing their hearts out.

In that moment, surrounded by thousands, they felt both a part of something much larger and intimately connected to one another.

During a slower song, 'Chiquitita', Maria whispered about a heartbreak she'd recently experienced. The lyrics seemed to speak directly to her, and Sophie squeezed her hand in comfort. Music, especially ABBA's, had that magical quality of being therapeutic, of echoing emotions so personal yet so universal.

The night came to a roaring climax with 'Waterloo', and the friends, drenched in sweat and exhilaration, joined the crowd in a standing ovation. As the lights came on and the crowd started to disperse, the group found a quiet spot outside the venue.

Under the starry sky, they made a promise. ABBA's music, with its timeless charm and infectious energy, would always be their anthem.

Whenever life took them on different paths, they'd play an ABBA song and be instantly transported back to this night, to their shared memories, to a time when all that mattered was the music and each other's company.

Years later, even as times changed and music evolved, the magic of that night remained a constant for them. Whenever they heard an ABBA song, no matter where they were, they'd smile, remembering the joy and camaraderie of that unforgettable concert.

52. The Joy of Roller Skating

Under the dim lights of the local roller rink, the soft hum of wheels gliding against the polished wooden floor merged with the lively beats of the decade's top hits. Laughter and chatter filled the air as families, both young and old, laced up their skates for an evening of pure, unadulterated joy.

Little Tommy, only six and donning his brand-new roller skates, hesitated at the rink's entrance. His big sister, Clara, grasped his hand reassuringly. "It's like dancing, Tommy! Just let the music guide you," she whispered. Taking a deep breath, Tommy stepped onto the rink, his initial wobbles soon transforming into confident strides.

At the center, Mrs. Henderson, the elderly neighbor who lived down the street, amazed everyone with her graceful moves.

Age hadn't dimmed her passion for skating, and the rink had always been her sanctuary. Watching her, young teens felt inspired and dared each other to mimic her elegant twirls.

Nearby, Mr. and Mrs. Garcia, who had met at this very roller rink years ago, rekindled their romance. Hand in hand, they skated to their song, the one that had played when Mr. Garcia had first asked his wife to skate with him. Their synchronized movements, a testament to their enduring bond, earned admiring glances from onlookers.

Outside the rink, parents and grandparents, some unable to skate due to age or ailment, cheered from the sidelines. They shared stories of their own roller-skating days, inspiring younger generations with tales of fun, falls, and friendships formed.

As the evening wore on and the music's tempo shifted to mellower tunes, skaters slowed, basking in the communal spirit that the rink fostered. It wasn't just about skating; it was about the shared moments, the connections made, and the memories etched in the heart.

As families headed home, the glow of the rink's neon sign cast a soft light on their contented faces. They carried with them the elation of the evening, a gentle reminder of simpler times and the sheer delight found in the company of loved ones and the joyous rhythm of roller skates.

53. Carol Burnett's Ear Tug

Every Saturday evening, like clockwork, Marjorie settled into her cozy armchair, ready for a dose of laughter courtesy of "The Carol Burnett Show." The skits made her belly laugh, sometimes causing her eyes to water, but it was the show's ending that always tugged at her heartstrings – Carol's signature ear tug.

It was a silent yet powerful gesture, a heartfelt shoutout to her beloved grandmother. Marjorie saw more in it, though. Every time Carol tugged her ear, Marjorie thought of her own daughter, Lucy, with whom she'd had a falling out years ago.

One particular evening, as Marjorie watched Carol bid adieu with the familiar ear tug, a realization washed over her.

The simple act was a bridge between generations, a silent message of love. Why couldn't she do the same? She longed to reconnect with Lucy, to mend the rift that had widened over the years.

Drawing inspiration from Carol's gesture, Marjorie penned a heartfelt letter to Lucy. She wrote of love, forgiveness, and understanding. And at the end of the letter, she drew a small sketch of a hand tugging an ear. It was her way of saying, "I'm thinking of you, and I love you."

Weeks passed, and then one evening, as Marjorie prepared for her weekly ritual of watching Carol Burnett, the doorbell rang. Standing there, holding the letter with the ear tug sketch, was Lucy. Without a word, they embraced, tears streaming down both their faces.

From that day on, every time Marjorie and Lucy said goodbye after a visit or ended a phone call, they tugged their ear. A simple, silent gesture, borrowed from a beloved comedian, became a symbol of enduring love between a mother and daughter.

54. The First Microwave Oven

The Thompsons were an ordinary family with the same weekday hustle as everyone else. Dad left early for work, Mom managed the house and their two kids, Lisa and Tommy, were always involved in after-school activities. This meant late nights and dinner preparations that often felt like a marathon.

It all changed on a Saturday in 1976. The family wandered into the local electronics store, their eyes catching the newest addition to modern living: the microwave oven. With its promise of meals in minutes, Mrs. Thompson was sold on the idea.

The kids were equally fascinated. "It looks like a TV for food," Tommy had remarked. That evening, as they set up the microwave in their kitchen, the air was thick with excitement. Mrs. Thompson decided to try out a simple meal - baked potatoes. In they went, and within minutes, out they came, perfectly cooked. The family was astounded.

Soon, the microwave became an integral part of the Thompson household. Morning oatmeal, afternoon popcorn snacks, and quick dinners became a breeze.

But it wasn't just about the convenience; it was about the moments it created. With less time spent on meal preparations, there was more time for family. Game nights became frequent, homework help was readily available, and bedtime stories grew longer.

Lisa began to learn new microwave recipes, making her a star during slumber parties. Tommy loved showing off the "space-age" technology to his friends. For Mr. and Mrs. Thompson, the joy was in watching their family bond over something so simple yet revolutionary.

The Thompsons' kitchen became a hub for neighbors too, curious about the marvel that was the microwave oven. Stories of the day and life advice were shared over quick meals and mugs of hot cocoa. It was a decade of change, and the microwave oven was at the heart of it all, turning mere meal prep into memorable moments.

The magic of the microwave wasn't just in its speedy cooking but in the togetherness it cooked up in homes everywhere. For the Thompsons, it was more than an appliance; it was the ingredient for countless cherished memories.

55. The Bicentennial Celebration

1976 was a special year for America, and for the Martins, it was the year they felt an even deeper connection to their country and community.

The anticipation built as the days led up to the Fourth of July. The entire town buzzed with excitement, lawns dotted with American flags, and storefronts decorated in red, white, and blue.

Mrs. Martin sewed matching outfits for the family: star-spangled vests for the boys and striped skirts for the girls. Their home's white picket fence received a fresh coat of paint, and a flag was proudly hoisted.

On the day of the celebration, the streets were lined with families. Children waved their little flags while vendors sold pinwheels, candies, and balloons.

The Martins found their spot on Main Street, their eyes all set on the grand parade. The rhythmic beats of the marching bands and the twirling batons of majorettes created an electric atmosphere.

Mr. Martin hoisted little Joey on his shoulders while Emma, with her face painted, danced to the music. The parade was a spectacular display of the community's spirit.

There were floats representing various eras of American history, and when the float commemorating the Declaration of Independence rolled by, a hush fell over the crowd, followed by an outburst of cheers.

As day turned to evening, families gathered at the town park. Picnic blankets were spread, and the tantalizing smell of barbecue filled the air. Children played catch while parents shared stories from their past, reconnecting with their roots.

Then, as the sky darkened, the moment everyone was waiting for arrived. Fireworks lit up the night, painting the sky with brilliant colors. Each explosion was met with gasps of wonder.

The Martins, hand in hand, looked up in awe, their hearts swelling with pride.

That Bicentennial Fourth of July wasn't just about commemorating 200 years of America's history; it was about communities and families like the Martins coming together, cherishing shared memories, and looking forward to the promise of the future. It was a day the Martins would fondly remember, a sparkling moment in the tapestry of their lives.

56. Cabbage Patch Kids Take Over

The '80s brought many exciting and unique fads, but none quite gripped the nation like the Cabbage Patch Kids. Every child wanted one, and stores couldn't keep them on the shelves.

Martha and Joseph, a loving couple in their 70s, heard whispers of this new craze from their neighbors, friends, and even on the evening news.

But it wasn't until their granddaughter Jenny shyly handed them her Christmas wish list, with "Cabbage Patch Doll" written in big, bold letters at the very top, that they truly understood the fervor.

Determined to bring joy to Jenny's Christmas, Martha and Joseph set out on what felt like an epic quest. They drove from store to store, standing in lines that snaked around corners, and even braved a snowy morning waiting outside a toy shop that rumored a new shipment.

One chilly December day, as they were sipping coffee in a little café, dejected from another unsuccessful hunt, Martha overheard a woman talking about a small store in a neighboring town that had just received a surprise delivery of the dolls.

With newfound hope, Joseph and Martha embarked on this lead. After a suspense-filled drive, they arrived at the quaint toy store. To their surprise, there were still a few Cabbage Patch Kids left!

As Martha lovingly selected a doll with brown curly hair, much like Jenny's, Joseph chatted with the store owner. The owner shared tales of parents and grandparents traveling from afar in search of these beloved dolls.

Christmas morning arrived, and the joy in Jenny's eyes as she unwrapped her Cabbage Patch Kid was unmatched. The doll's brown curls seemed to dance as Jenny twirled around in sheer happiness.

After all the excitement of the day had settled, Jenny climbed onto Martha's lap, her new doll cradled in her arms. "Thank you, Grandma. I love her," she whispered, a tear glistening in Martha's eye.

Years later, at a family gathering, a grown-up Jenny brought out the same Cabbage Patch doll, a little worn but still cherished. Holding the doll up, she said, "This isn't just a toy. This doll represents the lengths my grandparents went to make me happy. It's a symbol of their love."

That evening, as the family shared old stories and laughter, Martha and Joseph sat hand in hand, their hearts full, realizing that sometimes the smallest gestures leave the longest-lasting imprints on our souls.

57. Neil Armstrong's University Lecture

The auditorium was buzzing with excitement as students from all departments, not just engineering, filled the seats. The guest speaker was none other than Neil Armstrong, the first man to walk on the moon. For young Tom, an aspiring engineering student, this was not just another lecture; it was a dream come true.

As the lights dimmed, a hush settled over the audience. Neil Armstrong, with his signature modesty, walked onto the stage without any fanfare. He began recounting his experiences, not just the historic moon landing, but the years of preparation, the failures, the lessons, and the teamwork.

What struck Tom was not the tales of glory but the humility with which Armstrong spoke. He discussed the many engineers, scientists, and unsung heroes who never stepped onto the moon but made the journey possible.

He emphasized the importance of perseverance, collaboration, and pushing boundaries, saying, "It wasn't just one small step for a man but a giant leap for a dedicated team."

Armstrong's words were not just about space exploration. They were about life, about chasing dreams, and about the value of every individual in a team. Tom was spellbound, hanging on to every word.

After the lecture, Tom managed to approach Armstrong. With nervous energy, he said, "Mr. Armstrong, your journey and words today have inspired me deeply. I'm studying engineering, and I've always dreamt of being a part of something bigger than myself."

Armstrong, with a gentle smile, replied, "Then keep pushing forward, young man. Remember, it's not just about reaching your destination; it's about the journey and the people you work with. Make it count."

Years later, Tom, now a successful aerospace engineer, often recalled that day. Armstrong's words had not just inspired him but had given him a direction. He realized it wasn't just about the technicalities of engineering; it was about passion, teamwork, and leaving a mark for future generations.

On Tom's office wall, amidst various accolades, hung a framed picture of that day at the university, where a young student met his hero. It served as a constant reminder that one's humility and wisdom could inspire countless others to reach for the stars.

58. Steve Jobs and the Early Home Computer

The year was 1984, and in the Miller household, excitement was at an all-time high. Mr. Miller had just walked in, clutching a big box with the Apple logo. The family gathered around, their eyes wide with curiosity.

"Kids," Mr. Miller began, setting the box on the dining table, "This is the future. Meet our new Apple Macintosh."

Young Emma and Luke were instantly intrigued. With its sleek design and that cute little smile as it booted up, it was unlike anything they had seen. Emma was the first to ask, "Dad, can I try drawing on it?" Mr. Miller taught her how to use MacPaint, and soon, a digital masterpiece of the family dog adorned the screen.

Luke, ever the budding writer, was more interested in the word processing. He marveled at how he could edit sentences without white-out or starting over. "This is magic," he whispered.

Every evening, the Miller's dining room became a hub of exploration and creativity. Emma and Luke would take turns using the Macintosh, with Mr. Miller guiding them through its capabilities. They wrote stories, created artwork, and even played the occasional game.

More than the device itself, it was the world of possibilities the computer opened up that captured the children's imaginations. They realized that with this tool, they could create, innovate, and explore without limitations. It was a spark, a starting point to a lifelong journey.

Emma grew up to be a graphic designer, harnessing technology's power to create beautiful artworks. Luke became a software developer, constantly seeking ways to improve and innovate, just like the Apple team did with their early computers.

Years later, as adults, the siblings often reminisced about that magical evening when their father brought home the Macintosh. It wasn't just about the computer; it was about the promise of a brighter, limitless future.

In the heart of their family home, amidst photographs and cherished memories, stood the now vintage Apple Macintosh. A testament to a bygone era, and the beginning of the technological revolution that shaped their lives.

59. The Magic of Joe Frazier

It was a Sunday evening, and the dimly lit living room was filled with an air of anticipation. Young Timmy sat cross-legged on the floor, eyes glued to the flickering television screen. His grandfather sat behind him in his favorite armchair, the scent of his pipe filling the room.

"Who's fighting, Grandpa?" Timmy asked, unable to hide the excitement in his voice.

"That's Joe Frazier, kiddo," Grandpa replied, pointing to the robust figure on the screen. "One of the greatest boxers of our time."

As the match began, Timmy watched in awe. Frazier moved with a rhythm, a dance of power and poise. With each punch, each dodge, he seemed to tell a story. It wasn't just about the fight; it was about determination, resilience, and heart.

"Why does he fight, Grandpa?" Timmy pondered aloud during a round break.

Grandpa leaned forward, "Well, Timmy, some people fight to prove something, some for the thrill, but boxers like Joe? They fight because they have something inside them, a fire. They fight for honor, respect, and sometimes, they fight to find out who they truly are."

Timmy looked deep in thought. The match resumed, and Frazier's tenacity shone through. Even when knocked down, he got back up, face determined, gloves ready.

By the end, whether Frazier won or lost seemed secondary to the lesson he imparted.

A few days later, Grandpa found a makeshift boxing ring in the backyard, with Timmy practicing punches in the air. "Inspired by Frazier, huh?" Grandpa chuckled.

Timmy nodded, sweat dripping from his brow. "I want to be brave and strong like him. I want to learn about courage and confidence."

And so, with a pair of worn-out gloves from the attic and lessons from Grandpa, Timmy embarked on his boxing journey, not to fight others, but to discover the strength within himself, all thanks to the magic of Joe Frazier.

60. Happy Days on TV

The unmistakable tune of "Happy Days" echoed through the Johnson household every Tuesday evening. As the first notes played, the entire family would scramble from every corner of the house, congregating in the living room.

Little Danny, who usually couldn't sit still, would eagerly claim his spot on the floor, front and center. Grandpa Johnson, often reminiscing about his younger days, would settle into his favorite armchair with a smile. And the others would find their places on the couch, the scents of a finished dinner still wafting through the home.

The 1950s setting of the show was a nostalgic escape for the family. For Grandpa, it was a trip down memory lane. For the parents, it was a wholesome series full of life lessons they hoped Danny would pick up.

And for Danny, well, it was all about The Fonz. His eyes would light up whenever the leather-jacketed, motorcycle-riding character made an appearance. "Ayyy!" Danny would mimic, sending the room into peals of laughter.

For thirty minutes each week, the outside world faded away. There were no bills to worry about, no schoolwork to be done, just the heartwarming adventures of Richie, Potsie, Ralph, and of course, Fonzie.

As the credits rolled, Danny would jump up and make his way to Grandpa's chair. "Tell me again about the time you had your own 'Fonz' moment, Grandpa!" he'd beg, eyes twinkling. Grandpa would chuckle, ruffling Danny's hair, and the room would settle into another story, this time from their very own family history.

Flashback to the Flashy 1980's

61. The Thriller of 'Thriller'

Word on the street was that Michael Jackson was about to drop a new music video. Not just any video – but the most astounding, spine-chilling video the world would ever witness. Sara's living room was the designated gathering spot among her friends.

The clock neared the hour. Snacks scattered on the coffee table, the room was buzzing with excitement. Lisa was trying to predict the dance moves, while Tommy, a die-hard MJ fan, was practicing his moonwalk in a corner.

As the opening scene appeared, a hush descended. Michael's transformation into a werewolf made a few scream while others hid behind cushions. Sara's little brother Joey peeked from behind the sofa, eyes wide with a mix of fear and fascination.

But it was the dance sequence that truly stole the show. The synchronized steps of Jackson and his zombie crew were unlike anything anyone had seen.

Lisa was up, trying to mimic the iconic moves, pulling Tommy up with her. Soon enough, the entire room was on its feet, laughing, dancing, and getting entangled in the rhythm of 'Thriller.'

Once it ended, there was a collective sigh. Joey, with eyes sparkling, declared, "I wanna be just like Michael Jackson when I grow up!" The room erupted in laughter.

Over the years, many things changed, but that night remained etched in their memories. Whenever they heard 'Thriller,' smiles would instantly appear, recalling the evening filled with dance, laughter, and camaraderie. It was more than just a song; it was a testament to the power of music and the unforgettable moments it could create.

62. The Joy of the Walkman

The school hallways buzzed with chatter about TV shows, homework, and the latest music hits. But for Jake, the shy teenager with tousled hair and freckles, music was more than just a passing topic.

It was his escape.

Jake's world was changed one afternoon when he received a gift from his father: Sony's newest invention, the Walkman. With its sleek design and promise of personal music space, it was as if the future had landed in Jake's hands.

Clipping it to his belt, Jake ventured out, headphones on. As he pressed play, the world around him transformed. The street's regular hum faded away, replaced by the soulful voice of Stevie Wonder. For the first time, Jake felt like he was inside a cocoon of sound. Music flowed directly into his ears, making everything around him come alive. Trees danced, the streets pulsated, and the world moved in rhythm with his tunes.

At school, while others talked, Jake was wrapped up in his music world, exploring genres from rock to jazz. It became his companion during lonely lunch breaks, inspiring doodles in his notebook and daydreams of music-filled adventures.

One day, Lisa, a classmate, noticed Jake's toe-tapping and approached him. Curious, she wanted to listen in. Sharing one of the earbuds, they swayed to the melodic notes of The Beatles. It was the beginning of a beautiful friendship, bonded over shared music.

Decades later, Jake, now a radio DJ, would often share this story with his listeners. "The Walkman," he'd say, "taught me the power of music. It's not just about the notes; it's about the spaces it creates and the connections it fosters."

And so, in an era before streaming and smart devices, a simple portable cassette player opened up a world of wonder for a young boy, leading him to a lifelong love affair with music.

63. Family Game Night: Trivial Pursuit

The Williams' living room was always a hive of activity on Friday evenings. With a large colorful board sprawled out on their coffee table and stacks of cards arranged neatly, the scene was set for the highlight of their week: Trivial Pursuit night.

It began as an impromptu game session one evening when Mr. Williams brought home the game, thinking it might be an entertaining way to pass time. Little did he know, it would turn into a beloved ritual.

Sarah, the eldest at 16, always fancied herself the history buff. She would proudly answer questions about world events and ancient civilizations with an air of authority. David, 14, was the sports enthusiast.

He would light up whenever a sports question came up, rattling off statistics about players and tournaments. Young Amy, just 10, was surprisingly good at the arts and literature category. She'd often surprise them all with her knowledge of classic books and famous painters.

Mrs. Williams, a schoolteacher, loved the geography questions, often sharing anecdotes from her teaching days, while Mr. Williams, a mechanic, had an uncanny ability to guess answers even when he was unsure, bringing about roars of laughter with his wildly creative responses.

The beauty of these nights was the collective spirit of discovery and surprise. The little bets they'd make, like "If I get this right, you're doing the dishes!" or Sarah's attempts to mime out an answer she couldn't quite articulate.

On one special evening, as snow gently fell outside, the family was joined by Grandma Williams. With her added wealth of knowledge, she recounted tales that sprang from the questions, painting a vivid picture of the past and seamlessly bridging generations.

The night would usually end with everyone sprawled out, filled with snacks, Mr. Williams retelling his 'epic' game win from three weeks ago, and Amy dozing off on her mother's lap, the game box slightly askew.

For the Williams, these evenings were more than just game nights; they were moments frozen in time, snapshots of joy and togetherness that remained etched in their hearts, long after the game pieces were put away.

64. The Launch of the Space Shuttle Challenger

Mrs. Grant's fifth-grade classroom was buzzing with excitement that cold January morning. Today was special. Today was the day they were going to witness history. The classroom's old television, usually reserved for educational films, was now the center of attention. The Space Shuttle Challenger was about to launch.

"Quiet down, everyone!" Mrs. Grant beckoned, but her eyes sparkled with the same excitement that animated her students. "Let's watch."

Billy, an aspiring astronaut, sat at the edge of his seat, his eyes glued to the screen. To his left, Maria sketched the shuttle in her notebook, capturing its majesty before takeoff. The room was filled with a collective sense of wonder, a shared moment of anticipation.

As the countdown began, the classroom echoed the numbers. "Ten, nine, eight..." Their voices became a chorus of hope and expectation. With each decreasing number, their excitement swelled, hearts pounding in young chests.

And then, liftoff!

The Challenger soared, a beacon of human achievement and potential. The room erupted in applause and cheers, the children's faces illuminated by the TV's glow, reflecting the brightness of the shuttle.

"I want to be up there!" exclaimed Billy, eyes wide and full of stars.

"I'm going to design the next one!" declared Maria, her pencil dancing with newfound inspiration on the page.

Mrs. Grant looked around the room, taking in the awe-struck faces of her students. This moment, she knew, was more than just a historical event they were witnessing. It was a spark, a kindling of dreams and ambitions. The universe had suddenly expanded for them, and the sky was no longer the limit.

After the launch, the children excitedly discussed space, planets, and galaxies far away. The classroom felt alive with possibilities.

Years later, many from Mrs. Grant's class would remember that day, not just for the Challenger but for the boundless dreams it ignited. It was a day where imaginations soared, and the vastness of space felt just a little bit closer.

65. Bob Ross Paints a Happy Little World

Amidst the bustling city sounds and the never-ending worries of urban life, Clara's small apartment felt like an island of chaos. Lately, the world outside seemed so loud, the walls closing in with the weight of her own thoughts.

One evening, while aimlessly flipping through channels, a soft-spoken man with a halo of curly hair and a paintbrush in hand appeared on her screen. He was painting mountains, his voice calm and soothing, talking about "happy little trees" and "friendly clouds."

Captivated, Clara felt an unexpected calm wash over her. Bob Ross, with his gentle demeanor and kind words, painted not just scenes but a world full of hope and simplicity.

On a whim, Clara bought some basic painting supplies the next day. With Bob Ross's episodes as her guide, she began to paint. The bristles of the brush against the canvas were therapeutic. With each stroke, she felt her worries melt away, replaced by landscapes of her own creation.

Her apartment, once a symbol of her isolation, became a sanctuary filled with canvases of tranquil forests, serene lakes, and majestic mountains. Friends visiting Clara's apartment would often remark on the burst of color and life on her walls.

One evening, her young niece, Emily, stared at a painting of a serene lake with a mountain backdrop. "Aunt Clara, this feels like a hug," she whispered, encapsulating what Clara felt every time she picked up her brush.

Bob Ross, through his soothing words and strokes, had given Clara a gift. Not just the joy of painting, but the joy of rediscovering a world where every tree, cloud, and mountain had a story, a purpose. Through him, she had found a tranquil escape and a voice in the sweeping landscapes she created.

And so, in the heart of the city, amidst the noise and the rush, Clara painted a world of her own, one where every day was a good day to be alive.

66. Reagan's Tear-Down-This-Wall Speech

In a cozy living room in West Germany, the Müller family huddled around their television set. The anticipation was palpable. Their extended family, the Schultzes, sat beside them.

Although now sharing a living room, their lives had long been divided by the formidable Berlin Wall. It wasn't just bricks and mortar that separated them, but lifetimes of missed birthdays, anniversaries, and simple Sunday dinners.

Hans Müller remembered the tales of his grandparents' lively debates during family gatherings in Berlin before the wall. They'd argue about everything, from the best sausage recipe to politics.

But when the wall went up, those animated conversations came to an abrupt halt. Now, only letters relayed muted updates of life on the other side.

The room fell silent as President Ronald Reagan stood in front of the Brandenburg Gate, the iconic backdrop that symbolized so much pain and division for the family. "Mr. Gorbachev," Reagan's voice echoed, "tear down this wall!"

The weight of those words hung in the air. The room was thick with emotions, unshed tears glistening in the eyes of the elders. To young Petra Schultz, it was like watching a scene from a movie, but to her grandparents, it was hope vocalized.

Post-speech, over cups of steaming coffee and slices of Schwarzwalder Kirschtorte, the family discussed a world without the Wall. Imagining reunions, shared celebrations, and a future where the next generation wouldn't know the meaning of a divided Berlin.

Late into the night, as the family bid their goodbyes, Hans caught his cousin Friedrich's eye. They exchanged a knowing look, a shared hope, a bond once lost but now rediscovered.

The speech hadn't torn down the wall, but it had ignited a spark, a belief that walls, no matter how sturdy, couldn't divide hearts yearning to be united.

That evening, the families went to bed with dreams not of a divided East and West, but of a united Germany, a place where memories of separation would one day be just that – memories.

67. The First Personal Computers

Inside the cozy living room, Luke eagerly tore open the box labeled "Commodore 64", while his Grandpa Joe watched with a nostalgic glint in his eye.

"Hard to believe, Luke," Grandpa Joe mused, lifting a hefty keyboard from the box, "when I was your age, I typed my school essays on a typewriter. It clacked and dinged at the end of every line."

Luke laughed, "A typewrit-what?"

Grandpa chuckled, "You'd think it was an antique!"

Together, they navigated the maze of cables, buttons, and plugs. Each successful beep from the computer drew smiles and high-fives. Grandpa Joe recounted tales of a world where answering a phone meant twirling a rotary dial, while Luke imagined video games he'd play on this new computer.

As dusk approached, they finally managed to display a simple pixelated game on the screen. With the room illuminated only by the computer's glow, Grandpa tried his hand at the game, his fingers clumsily navigating the controls, causing both of them to erupt in laughter.

Sitting side by side on the floor, munching on a shared bowl of popcorn, they relished the simple joy of new discoveries and memories of a world that once was. Their shared afternoon wasn't about a computer; it was about the timeless joy of shared experiences across generations.

68. Paul Newman's Philanthropy

One sunny morning, Marge and Ted sat in their modest kitchen, sharing a light salad lunch. The star of the meal was the tangy dressing from a bottle adorned with Paul Newman's face.

"You know," Marge said, taking another bite, "this dressing isn't just tasty. Newman donates all the post-tax profits to charity!"

Ted looked intrigued, "Really? From just salad dressing?"

It wasn't long before the couple, inspired by Paul's venture, began brainstorming. With Ted's talent for crafting and Marge's knack for baking, they introduced their neighborhood to "Ted's Wooden Creations" and "Marge's Delightful Pastries."

Their quaint garage transformed into a bustling workshop. The air was always filled with the sweet scent of fresh pies and the gentle rasping of wood. They laughed, fumbled, learned, but most importantly, they loved the joy it brought them and their community.

As the months went by, their creations became the talk of the town. And true to the inspiration they derived from Newman's Own, they decided to donate a portion of their earnings to the local children's hospital.

Each month, when they handed over the donation, they felt an immense sense of fulfillment. It wasn't just about the money; it was about the love they put into their crafts and the love they gave back to the community.

One day, a young mother approached Marge at their stall, her eyes brimming with tears. "Your donation helped my little girl get the treatment she needed," she whispered, holding Marge's hands tightly.

For Marge and Ted, that moment encapsulated everything. They might have been retired, but they discovered a new purpose.

On chilly evenings, they'd often sit on their porch, reminiscing about times gone by, about records and drive-in movies.

But the topic they loved revisiting the most was the day they decided to start their venture, inspired by a simple bottle of salad dressing. It was proof that it's never too late to make a change, to bring smiles, and to sprinkle a little kindness in the world.

69. Glam Rock and Hair Bands

It was 1986, and the evening was awash with neon lights and the electric thrum of excitement. Outside the city's largest arena, queues formed as fans chattered animatedly, donning their best glam attire. Among them were Jess and her crew, each decked out in glittery outfits, wild hairstyles towering to the sky.

"You think they'll play 'Wild Nights' tonight?" Jess asked, adjusting her oversized hoop earrings.

"They have to!" replied Tim, his own hair sprayed to perfection. "It's their biggest hit!"

Amidst the laughter and playful banter, the group shared stories of previous concerts, reliving the moments of adrenaline and joy. These nights were their escape, a time when nothing mattered but the music, the lights, and the shared experience of being young.

Inside, the arena transformed into a sensory explosion. Lasers painted the crowd, strobe lights punctuated the rhythm, and the earth-shaking roar of the electric guitars announced the beginning of the concert.

As the curtain lifted, there they were - their favorite glam rock band in all their glory. Electric riffs echoed as the music took over, drawing everyone into its embrace.

Jess and her friends danced, sang, and lost themselves in the music, letting go of all inhibitions. Each song became an anthem of their youth, a promise of endless possibilities. The pulsating drums, the fiery solos, and the mesmerizing vocals were an invitation to a world where dreams and reality collided.

During the ballad, Tim leaned over, "These are the moments, Jess. The ones we'll talk about when we're old and grey."

And they did. Decades later, Jess, now a grandmother, would often recount the tales of her glam rock days to her grandchildren.

The neon, the wild hair, the boundless energy of youth. Through her stories, the spirit of those days lived on, connecting generations through the universal language of music and the memory of a night when anything seemed possible.

70. Tom Brokaw and the Greatest Generation

The sun was setting, casting a golden hue throughout the living room where Robert sat, remote in hand. Flipping through channels, his eyes settled on a familiar face. Tom Brokaw, whose trusted voice had narrated many a historical event, was on screen discussing World War II veterans.

Robert leaned forward, the weight of memories pressing on him. Clips of old soldiers, men like him, recounting their stories filled the screen. The raw emotions, the courage, and the shared experiences resonated with him.

His granddaughter, Emma, walked in, her curiosity piqued. "Grandpa, isn't that when you were in the war?"

Robert nodded, eyes still fixed on the TV. A particular story, a tale of camaraderie amidst chaos, mirrored one of his own. The barriers he'd built over the years, the stories locked away, seemed to waver.

Emma sensed an opening. Sitting down beside him, she gently prodded, "Did something like that happen to you?"

Taking a deep breath, Robert began to speak, sharing tales of brave comrades, of near misses, and moments that defined his youth. He talked of friendships forged in the crucible of war and the resilience of a generation that endured so much.

As he spoke, his family gathered, captivated by his recollections. For the first time, they glimpsed the young soldier that once was, understanding the man before them a little better.

Inspired by Brokaw's interviews, Robert's memories bridged the chasm of time, forging new connections with his loved ones. That evening, history wasn't just something in a book or on a TV screen; it was alive, breathing, and sitting right there in their living room.

71. Mother Teresa's Visit to America

The excitement in the O'Reilly household was palpable. Mother Teresa, the living saint from Calcutta, was visiting New York. The news buzzed with her images, those gentle eyes and warm smiles offering solace to everyone she met.

Lena, the matriarch, watched with her children, John and Maria, as the petite nun with white and blue robes moved gracefully amidst the skyscrapers and bustling streets of New York. Mother Teresa's message was simple: love and serve the poorest of the poor.

"That's what real kindness is," Lena whispered, wiping away a tear.

John, an inquisitive teenager, questioned, "Mom, why do people love her so much?"

Lena responded, "Because she sees beauty in places where most of us only see despair. She reminds us of the good we can do."

Maria, the younger sibling, chimed in, "Can we help people too?"

And so, the seed was planted.

The following Saturday, the O'Reillys set out to their local soup kitchen. John, initially hesitant, was soon dishing out meals, laughing with the people, and listening to their stories. Maria, with her infectious enthusiasm, drew smiles from even the most downtrodden.

Lena watched her children, pride filling her heart. This wasn't just a one-time event. Week after week, the family found themselves at the soup kitchen, helping out, meeting other volunteers, and forming bonds with those they served.

Years later, John and Maria would often recall that pivotal moment, Mother Teresa's visit. It wasn't just the memory of a famous figure visiting their city. It was the realization that they too had a role in making their community a better place.

And it all began in their cozy living room, with the image of a diminutive nun on TV, reminding them of the immense power of love and compassion.

72. The Wit of Johnny Carson

In the heart of a small town, Helen and Thomas had a cherished nightly ritual. With their two mugs of decaf coffee in hand, they'd snuggle up on their worn-out couch, ready for their favorite time of the night—watching "The Tonight Show Starring Johnny Carson."

They'd been watching Johnny since their early days of dating. Thomas had wooed Helen with his impression of Johnny's comedic style, while Helen, always quick-witted herself, often threw back retorts that could rival any of Carson's guests.

Every night, as the familiar theme song played, they'd squeeze each other's hands in giddy anticipation. Carson's monologues, with his sharp wit and impeccable timing, had the couple bursting into fits of laughter. They'd often joke that Carson was their nightly therapy, chasing away the day's worries with his playful banter.

On nights when a particularly memorable joke or skit aired, the couple would relive it the next day, mimicking Carson's voice or reenacting a funny scene, much to the amusement of their neighbors and friends.

But beyond the laughs, their shared moments watching Carson symbolized something deeper. During tough times—whether it was financial strain, health issues, or the challenges of raising two kids—it was their shared laughter, their mutual adoration for Johnny's comedic genius, that pulled them closer together.

Over the years, as their children grew and moved away, and their home echoed with the silence of an empty nest, Johnny's show remained a constant. His playful humor, the parade of guests, and the sheer joy of the live audience, filled their home with warmth.

One evening, as they laughed at another one of Johnny's antics, Helen turned to Thomas, her eyes gleaming with tears of joy. "You know, Tom, life's been full of ups and downs. But these nights, with you, Johnny, and our cups of coffee, they're my favorite."

Thomas squeezed her hand, smiling, "Mine too, dear. Here's to many more nights with Mr. Carson."

And so, through the years, the couple's nightly ritual continued, a testament to shared joys, enduring love, and the timeless wit of Johnny Carson.

73. The Mt. St. Helens Miracle

The Martins were a close-knit family, always seeking out the next adventure. Every summer, their tradition was to pack their station wagon and head off to a beautiful camping spot. This year's destination: the picturesque surroundings of Mt. St. Helens.

However, as the date of their trip drew closer, a restless unease settled over Mrs. Martin. Each night, she had vivid dreams of the mountain, with ash-filled skies and chaos all around. These dreams felt oddly real, unlike any she'd had before. She tried to dismiss them as nerves, but the unsettling feeling persisted.

One evening, as the family sat around the dinner table, Mrs. Martin hesitated, then said, "I've been having these strange dreams about our trip. I can't shake off the feeling. Would you all mind if we changed our plans?"

Young Tommy, always eager for a new place to explore, quickly said, "How about Eagle Creek? We've never camped by a stream before!"

Mr. Martin, noticing his wife's distress, nodded in agreement. "Eagle Creek it is."

The family had a wonderful time at Eagle Creek, catching fish, sharing stories, and basking in the beauty of nature. But on the morning of May 18, 1980, as they sat around the campfire, the ground shook violently. They looked up in horror as a large plume of ash clouded the distant horizon.

Rushing to their car radio, they heard the news. Mt. St. Helens had erupted. The very campsite they'd intended to stay at was now under a thick blanket of ash.

The gravity of their near miss weighed heavily on them. That night, as they huddled together, Mrs. Martin whispered, "It's as if something was watching over us, urging us to change our plans."

Years later, the story of their "Mt. St. Helens Miracle" became a family legend. While they never truly understood why Mrs. Martin felt that compelling urge to change destinations, they remained eternally grateful for the divine intervention or sixth sense that kept them safe.

74. Bob Ross Paints a Happy Little World

Amidst the pastel wallpaper of her grandmother's living room, Maria sat, a weight heavy on her heart. Having recently lost her job and going through a rough breakup, the world felt gray. Her grandma, sensing Maria's despair, clicked on the TV, hoping to find a distraction. As the screen warmed, the soothing voice of Bob Ross echoed in the room.

"There are no mistakes," he murmured, dabbing his brush gently onto the canvas, "just happy little accidents."

Maria was entranced. Here was a man, with a mop of curly hair and a gentle demeanor, painting a vibrant world filled with cheerful trees and serene waters. Each stroke he made brought life, color, and positivity. For the first time in weeks, Maria felt a smile tugging at her lips.

After the episode ended, Maria's grandmother, sensing an opportunity, fetched an old canvas and a set of paints from her attic. "Why don't you give it a try?" she nudged.

A bit hesitant at first, Maria soon found herself immersed in a world of colors. With each stroke, she felt the weight lifting off her shoulders.

Her worries transformed into swirling skies and her sadness into blooming meadows. Bob Ross, with his encouraging words, had ignited a passion within her she never knew existed.

Days turned into weeks, and Maria's living room transformed into a mini studio. Her paintings, filled with vibrant colors and emotions, began to adorn the walls of her friends and family. They became a testament to her journey from despair to joy.

Years later, Maria would often tell the tale of the day she discovered Bob Ross. How, during her darkest days, a man with a calm voice and a paintbrush showed her the beauty in every "happy little accident."

75. Teen Movies and Coming of Age

The aroma of buttery popcorn filled the air as Jane, Michael, and Clara settled onto the worn-out couch in Jane's basement. It was their monthly movie night, and tonight's choice was the cult classic, "The Breakfast Club."

As the film rolled, the room was filled with bouts of laughter, knowing nods, and reminiscent sighs. Each character on the screen - the athlete, the princess, the brain, the criminal, and the basket case - seemed to evoke a personal memory from one of the friends.

"I was totally Brian," Michael confessed, adjusting his glasses, "Always buried in books, hoping to meet everyone's expectations." Clara and Jane chuckled, recalling the time he had recited the entire periodic table during lunch.

Clara sighed dreamily as Molly Ringwald's character, Claire, graced the screen. "You know, I felt a lot like Claire. Trying so hard to fit into that 'perfect' mold." She twirled a strand of her hair, lost in memories of high school dances and first dates.

Jane laughed, "And guess who I was? Bender! Always the rebel, always questioning authority." Michael smirked, "And always in detention."

The film's heartfelt moments, coupled with its humor, made the trio reflect on their own teenage journeys. Each of them had faced their own challenges, their own moments of self-doubt, and their own victories.

When the movie ended, Jane pulled out a shoebox from under the coffee table. It was filled with high school memorabilia - photographs, diary entries, ticket stubs.

They took turns sharing their keepsakes, reminiscing about old crushes, high school dances, and even those awkward moments that now only made them laugh.

As the evening wound down, they realized that while movies could take them back in time, it was their shared memories and enduring friendship that truly made those bygone days golden.

76. VCR and Movie Rentals

The aroma of buttery popcorn filled the air as Jane, Michael, and Clara settled onto the worn-out couch in Jane's basement. It was their monthly movie night, and tonight's choice was the cult classic, "The Breakfast Club."

As the film rolled, the room was filled with bouts of laughter, knowing nods, and reminiscent sighs. Each character on the screen - the athlete, the princess, the brain, the criminal, and the basket case - seemed to evoke a personal memory from one of the friends.

"I was totally Brian," Michael confessed, adjusting his glasses, "Always buried in books, hoping to meet everyone's expectations." Clara and Jane chuckled, recalling the time he had recited the entire periodic table during lunch.

Clara sighed dreamily as Molly Ringwald's character, Claire, graced the screen. "You know, I felt a lot like Claire. Trying so hard to fit into that 'perfect' mold." She twirled a strand of her hair, lost in memories of high school dances and first dates.

Jane laughed, "And guess who I was? Bender! Always the rebel, always questioning authority." Michael smirked, "And always in detention."

The film's heartfelt moments, coupled with its humor, made the trio reflect on their own teenage journeys. Each of them had faced their own challenges, their own moments of self-doubt, and their own victories.

As the final scene unfolded, with the characters leaving the school in their separate ways, the trio fell into a reflective silence. Michael broke it, "Isn't it amazing how films like these still resonate? Even after all these years?"

Jane nodded, "It's because everyone has a story, a chapter from their past they can link to these characters."

Clara, always the poet among them, added, "And just like a movie, life has its scenes, but friendships like ours, they're the timeless soundtrack that keeps playing on."

77. The Magic of the Perm: A Mother-Daughter Bonding Experience

"Oh, come on, honey! It'll be fun!" Clara urged, her eyes gleaming with excitement as she held up a 1980s beauty magazine showcasing a model with luscious, curly locks. Her teenage daughter, Lily, looked skeptical, her own straight hair cascading over her shoulders.

"I don't know, Mom," Lily hesitated, eyeing the perms of the past, "Are you sure about this?"

Clara laughed, remembering her own first perm. "It's a rite of passage! Trust me," she winked, "It's magical!"

So, on a lazy Saturday, the duo found themselves in Mrs. Henderson's cozy little salon. With old-timey radio tunes playing softly in the background, Clara watched her daughter's transformation begin. The familiar scent of the solution, the rollers, the hairnet - it all took Clara down memory lane.

Lily squirmed a bit, impatient. "How much longer?"

Clara chuckled, "Beauty takes time." She shared stories of her own perm adventures, the friends she went with, and the reactions they received. The tales of high school dances, movie nights, and slumber parties painted a vivid picture of a time gone by.

As the afternoon sun waned, Mrs. Henderson finally unveiled Lily's new curly mane. Lily's eyes widened in awe, her fingers running through the bouncy curls. She twirled, watching her reflection, a mix of amusement and appreciation in her gaze.

Clara clapped, "You look stunning! Just like the magazine!"

Lily giggled, "It's... different, but I like it!" She paused, her face softening, "Thanks, Mom. For this and the stories. I feel closer to you somehow."

Clara hugged her tightly, "It's the magic of the perm, honey."

They left the salon, their laughter echoing in the fading light, a shared experience weaving a bond even stronger than before.

78. The Fax Machine Revolution

"It's the future, Clara!" exclaimed John, gesturing dramatically towards the sleek new fax machine occupying a prominent space on the counter. The family-owned business, Bennett & Co., had been running smoothly for years, but this was the promise of a new era.

Clara was skeptical. "I don't understand, John. Why can't we stick with the good old postal service?"

John laughed. "Just watch!"

Soon, orders were coming in faster, operations streamlined, and response times halved. The little machine buzzed and whirred, spitting out paper with messages from businesses across the country. It was mesmerizing.

One day, as Clara was about to close up, the fax machine sprang to life. Curious, she picked up the incoming message. Her eyes widened in surprise. "To Bennett & Co.," it read. "Remember our summers at Lake Erie? Would love to reconnect. - Michael."

Clara gasped. Michael had been a dear childhood friend, but they had lost touch over the decades. Their families had shared countless picnics, boat rides, and laughter at Lake Erie.

Excitedly, she dialed the number listed on the fax. A familiar voice answered, "Bennett & Co., Michael speaking."

"Michael! It's Clara!"

The next hour was filled with joyful reminiscing and catch-ups. Michael had set up a business not too far away and had chanced upon their name while updating his contact list. The fax machine had bridged a gap widened by time and distance.

The Bennett family soon found themselves at a reunion picnic, the shores of Lake Erie echoing with laughter just like the old times. The kids listened, wide-eyed, to tales of adventures and antics, while the adults cherished the rekindling of cherished friendships.

Back at Bennett & Co., Clara glanced at the fax machine, a smile playing on her lips. "Alright, John," she conceded, "maybe it is the future."

And indeed, it was a future filled with unexpected joys and reconnections. The fax machine had not just revolutionized their business, but it had also magically rewoven the fabric of their past.

79. The Wonder of 'The Little Mermaid'

In the dimly lit living room, the VHS tape slid into the player, and soon, the enchanting underwater world of Ariel and her friends unfolded on the screen. Sarah and Jake, two energetic siblings, sat spellbound, their eyes wide with wonder. Beside them, their grandparents, Mr. and Mrs. Thompson, watched the film and the children with equal fascination.

Mrs. Thompson leaned over, whispering, "You know, this story reminds me of an old tale I heard as a child." Sarah, her attention slightly diverted, asked, "Really, Grandma?"

Mr. Thompson nodded, his face illuminated by the flickering TV light. "Oh yes, long before Ariel sang about wanting to be 'part of your world,' there was a story about a young mermaid who traded her voice for love. I believe it was by Hans Christian Andersen."

Jake's curiosity peaked. "Did she have a friend like Flounder and Sebastian?"

Mrs. Thompson chuckled. "Perhaps not exactly. But her story was filled with bravery, love, and sacrifice."

The movie played on, but during the quieter moments, the grandparents wove in tidbits from the original tale, drawing parallels and contrasts, making the watching experience richer and deeper.

By the movie's end, Sarah and Jake weren't just enthralled by the adventures of Ariel; they were wrapped up in the shared stories and warmth of the room.

The next day, Jake was found sketching mermaids and ships, while Sarah sat close to her grandmother, an old book open between them, diving into the original mermaid tale.

As the sun cast a golden hue through the window, Mr. Thompson put an arm around his wife. Together, they watched the grandchildren, their voices a soft harmony of laughter and discovery, a simple moment making it clear that stories, old and new, have a way of bringing hearts together.

80. The Home Fitness Revolution

The Johnson family living room had witnessed countless gatherings, movie nights, and birthday parties. But one Saturday morning, it was transformed into something entirely different—a home gym.

Mrs. Johnson proudly held up a set of VHS tapes she had recently purchased. "Families that sweat together, stay together!" she declared with enthusiasm. "Introducing the 'Ultimate Fitness at Home' series!"

Mr. Johnson looked skeptical, "Are we trading our popcorn nights for push-up nights now?"

Their teenage daughter, Lisa, examined the tape cover, "Look at those neon leotards and leg warmers! Totally rad!"

And so, the fitness journey began. Every morning, the VCR whirred to life, casting energetic instructors onto the TV screen, leading the family through an array of aerobics, dance routines, and yoga stretches.

The living room became a maze of flailing arms, mis-timed jumps, and stifled giggles. Mr. Johnson, attempting to follow along, often found himself two steps behind, while their younger son, Tommy, improvised with exaggerated moves, making Lisa burst into laughter.

One day, as Mrs. Johnson tried to balance in a challenging yoga pose, she lost her footing and landed right into the couch pillows. Instead of feeling embarrassed, she burst out laughing, setting off a chain reaction of chuckles around the room.

Despite the occasional mishaps and varied coordination levels, the sessions became something the family looked forward to. Not just for the exercise, but for the shared moments of joy, light-heartedness, and the collective goal of trying something new.

Soon, neighbors joined in, turning Saturday mornings into community workout sessions, full of camaraderie and playful competition.

As the tapes played on day after day, the living room, with its worn-out carpet and cozy corners, wasn't just a place of relaxation anymore. It became a symbol of unity, growth, and the simple pleasure of moving to the rhythm of life.

Rewinding to the 1990s!

81. The Launch of the Hubble Space Telescope

The walls of Mrs. Eleanor "Ellie" Mitchell's living room were lined with shelves upon shelves of books. Stacks of National Geographic magazines, old textbooks, and curiously enough, a large collection of space-themed puzzles.

Eleanor had retired five years ago after spending 35 years teaching middle school science.

Those years had been punctuated by the joy of watching young minds grasp the wonders of the universe. But as the years of retirement settled in, Ellie often felt her own sense of wonder diminishing.

One evening, while sipping her chamomile tea, Eleanor tuned into the news, adjusting the bunny ears atop her old television. The newscaster was enthusiastically detailing the imminent launch of the Hubble Space Telescope.

Ellie's heart fluttered. She remembered teaching her students about space telescopes and the potential they had for reshaping our understanding of the cosmos.

In the weeks that followed, Eleanor eagerly awaited news of the Hubble. She would often bring out her old telescope and gaze up at the night sky from her backyard, imagining the marvels the Hubble would soon uncover.

Her curiosity was infectious. Neighbors, young and old, would often join her, laying out blankets and gazing upwards, sharing whispered stories about stars and galaxies.

Then, the day came. The first images from Hubble were released. Eleanor watched, her heart in her throat, as mesmerizing images of nebulae, stars, and distant galaxies filled her screen. These were parts of the universe she had only read about in textbooks, and now, they were laid out in stunning detail before her.

The Pillars of Creation, as one image was named, was particularly enchanting. Towering columns of interstellar dust and gas, light-years tall, birthing new stars.

Ellie felt like she was seeing the universe with fresh eyes, the same awe she had felt as a young teacher. And she knew she couldn't keep this feeling to herself.

With renewed energy, Ellie started a weekly Astronomy Club in her neighborhood. Kids, parents, and fellow retirees gathered in her living room, poring over Hubble's latest captures, building models, and discussing the wonders of space.

During one session, a young girl named Lucy whispered to

Eleanor, "I want to be an astronomer when I grow up." Eleanor smiled, her eyes glistening, "The universe is yours to explore, Lucy."

Late at night, after her sessions, Eleanor would sometimes sit by her window, staring up at the sky, feeling an overwhelming connection to the vastness above.

Thanks to Hubble, not only had she rediscovered her passion, but she had also ignited that same spark in others. The universe felt a little bit closer, and the wonders within it, infinitely more personal.

82. The World of Windows 95

The Miller family home was always filled with the usual hustle and bustle. Breakfasts rushed before school, shared tales of the day over dinner, and late-night TV sessions. But on one peculiar Saturday, a fresh energy electrified the air. A big box arrived, bearing the logo "Windows 95."

Dad, always eager to keep up with the times, had decided to upgrade their home computer. "It's a new world," he'd say, "and we're going to be a part of it!" The kids, Sarah and Jamie, exchanged excited glances as the computer booted up, displaying the now-iconic start-up screen.

When the soft chime filled the room, indicating the computer was ready, Jamie gasped, "It's got color!" Sarah chuckled, rolling her eyes, "Of course, goofball. Everything's more colorful now."

Then came the magic moment. The family watched in amazement as Dad clicked on the new 'Internet Explorer' icon.

A series of beeps and tones emitted from the bulky modem, each sound seemingly a step closer to the vast expanse of the World Wide Web. When the final triumphant tone sounded, they were connected.

The Miller's living room was suddenly a gateway to the world. Sarah typed in the name of her favorite band and gasped as pictures, interviews, and fan sites sprawled out before her. Jamie, a budding scientist, found a website about dinosaurs, eyes widening as animations brought the prehistoric creatures to life.

Mrs. Miller, a librarian, marveled at the digital libraries and databases. "So many books! So much knowledge at our fingertips," she whispered, feeling the world shrink just a bit.

And then, something truly magical happened. Dad typed in a familiar last name and city into a chatroom. The screen buzzed, and then words began appearing.

"Is this the Miller family from Elm Street? It's your cousin Larry from Australia!" The room filled with gasps and wide eyes. The Internet wasn't just a tool; it was a bridge connecting family separated by oceans.

Days turned into weeks, and the Millers found their lives intertwined with the web. Homework, hobbies, family connections – all enhanced by this digital marvel.

In the years that followed, technology continued its rapid march forward. But for the Millers, it was that Saturday morning that stood out. Sometimes, on cozy winter nights, they'd huddle together, recalling the joy of discovering that new universe.

Sarah reminiscing about her first online fan group, Jamie chuckling about the silly sounds of the modem, and Mrs. Miller lost in the memory of the digital books she'd discovered.

And they'd all smile, thinking about Cousin Larry's surprise message, a warm reminder of the day their world expanded in ways they'd never imagined.

83. The Queen of Talk Shows: Oprah Winfrey

Janet sat on her old floral couch, a cup of tea in hand, the room illuminated only by the soft glow of the television screen. Every afternoon, she made it a point to watch "The Oprah Winfrey

Show." It was her small slice of solace in a world that often felt overwhelming.

One particular episode grabbed her attention. Oprah was featuring women who had taken leaps of faith to pursue their passions, irrespective of age or circumstance. Each guest shared their story, their struggles, and the transformative power of believing in oneself.

Janet hung onto every word, tears streaming down her face. For years, she had suppressed her dream of starting a bakery, always finding reasons why it wasn't the "right time."

The stories resonated deep within Janet. She saw herself in each of these women, their hesitations, their fears. But more importantly, she saw the possibility of a different life, one where she chased after her dreams with as much vigor as she put into her daily tasks.

Late into the night, Janet scribbled down ideas in her worn-out notebook: possible names for her bakery, recipes she wanted to try, and places she could rent. The early morning sun peeked through her curtains as she crafted a plan.

Months turned into years, and with hard work, Janet's bakery became a reality. The aroma of fresh pastries wafted through the town square, drawing in locals and tourists alike. Inside, a framed photo of Oprah adorned the wall, a silent testament to the power of inspiration.

On cool evenings, when the bakery had quieted down, Janet would often sit by the window, gazing at the families enjoying her creations. She'd smile, thinking of that fateful episode, the nudge she had needed.

Every now and then, a young woman would walk in, eyes full of dreams, and Janet would share her tale, filling the air with hope, ambition, and the rich aroma of freshly baked bread.

84. The Rise of Home Video Gaming

The room hummed with excitement as young Max and Sophie set up the brand new video game console, their eager fingers deftly connecting cables. Their Grandpa Joe, observing from his armchair, shook his head in bemusement. "Back in my day, we had marbles and wooden tops," he chuckled.

Sophie shot him a playful smirk. "Want to try, Grandpa? It's not just for kids, you know!"

Joe hesitated. The controllers seemed too intricate, the screen too dynamic. But seeing the hopeful eyes of his grandchildren, he decided to give it a shot. "Alright, just go easy on this old-timer."

The first few attempts were predictably disastrous. The character he was controlling kept falling into pits or running into obstacles. But Max and Sophie cheered him on, offering advice and strategy.

Soon, something incredible began to happen. The three of them, with generations between them, were laughing and playing together as if there was no age gap at all. Grandpa Joe, with each passing game, was not just adapting but becoming genuinely competitive.

The joy in his eyes was evident, not just from the thrill of the game but from this newfound connection with his grandchildren.

Weekends at Grandpa's turned into marathon gaming sessions. Neighbors and friends would often peek in to find the trio engrossed in their digital quests, Joe's booming laughter echoing every time he managed a win.

One warm evening, as they sat together, snacking on buttered popcorn, Joe began to describe the thrill of playing with spinning tops in the alleys, the precision it required, and the satisfaction of a win. The children listened with rapt attention, visualizing their grandpa as a young boy, playing in a world without screens.

Weekends at Grandpa's turned into a delightful blend of the digital and the past. The room, filled with the comforting scent of old books, the warmth of Joe's vintage rug, and the electronic chirps of the video game, became a haven of intergenerational bonding.

And as winter turned to spring, outside the window, amidst the familiar landscape of the neighborhood, a small patch of the garden transformed into a makeshift marble ring, a nod to the games of yesteryears, and a tribute to the timeless bond between a grandpa and his grandchildren.

85. The Beanie Baby Phenomenon

There was a peculiar fever that gripped the Johnson family in the late '90s. It wasn't the flu, nor was it the chickenpox. It was Beanie Babies!

Mom was the first to get bitten by the Beanie bug. It started innocently enough with "Patti the Platypus." Soon, the dining table was teeming with creatures of all shapes and sizes, from "Legs the Frog" to "Chocolate the Moose."

Dad, initially skeptical, found himself scouring yard sales for the elusive "Peanut the Royal Blue Elephant." And let's not even mention Grandma, who, despite her penchant for misplacing her glasses, could spot a "Princess Diana Bear" from a mile away.

The kids, Jake and Emma, were the designated Beanie Baby hunters on every family road trip. Whether it was a gas station or a small town thrift shop, no stone was left unturned. Their shared goal? Find the rarest Beanie Baby and earn the title of "Ultimate Beanie Boss" within the family.

Sundays were "Beanie Trade Days" at the Johnson house. Each member came with their duplicates and a list of desired Beanie Babies. They'd haggle, negotiate, and sometimes even stage dramatic performances, all in good fun, to sway the trade in their favor.

One summer evening, as they sat in the backyard, their collection spread out on picnic blankets, the sun casting long shadows over their precious trove, Jake broke the silence, "You know, it's not really about the Beanies, is it?"

Emma giggled, holding up "Bubbles the Fish," "Well, partly it is. Look at this cutie!" But her smile softened as she added, "But mostly, it's about us, isn't it? The hunts, the trades, the laughs..."

Dad, ever the joker, chimed in, holding a bear aloft, "And the kingdom I'll build with my army of Beanies!"

They all laughed, and in that golden hour, surrounded by a world of plush toys, the Johnsons realized the true treasures were the memories they were weaving together.

86. The Macarena Wedding

It was Amelia and Peter's wedding day, and the reception hall was filled with laughter, clinking glasses, and the occasional happy tear. The DJ was playing a mix of modern hits and old-school classics, creating a dance floor that ebbed and flowed with all age groups.

Then, that unmistakable beat started, prompting giggles and whispers across the room. "Oh no, not the Macarena!" someone exclaimed, but in seconds, the infectious tune had everyone tapping their feet.

The younger generation seemed almost bemused by the dance's simple choreography, while the adults joyously took their positions, ready to revisit their past.

But then, stealing the spotlight, Grandma Ellie, with her silver hair and twinkling eyes, sprang up from her chair. She confidently took center stage, her hands quickly going to her hips as she started the familiar moves.

There were gasps of surprise and roars of laughter as she led the way. From cousins to uncles, everyone joined in, creating a ripple of synchronized moves that filled the entire hall. Even little Timmy, who had previously been too shy to dance, couldn't resist joining the spectacle.

As the final notes played, the crowd erupted in applause, with Grandma Ellie taking a theatrical bow, a playful smirk on her face.

From that day on, every family wedding had its own Macarena moment. It didn't matter if it was considered outdated or if other, newer dances had taken the limelight. The Macarena had sealed its place in family lore.

At Uncle Robert's wedding, there was even a "Macarena Dance-Off" where two teams competed for the title of "Macarena Master." And who was the judge? None other than Grandma Ellie, of course!

Years later, during family gatherings, the tale of the Macarena Wedding would be narrated and re-narrated, each time with added flair and drama.

And as night descended, the familiar tune would play, and young and old would once again join hands, laughing and dancing together, celebrating the joy of family and the unexpected moments that bring them closer.

87. Julia Roberts' Smile

Tom sat alone in his dim living room, the glow of the television casting a familiar blue hue. On the screen, Julia Roberts laughed,

her infectious smile lighting up the scene in "Pretty Woman."
Tom's heart ached, for that smile was so like Eleanor's—the
playful curve of her lips, the way her eyes crinkled at the corners.

They'd seen this movie in theaters back in the '90s. Eleanor had
leaned over, whispering, "She reminds me of our first date,
remember? I wore that red dress just like hers." And indeed, she
had. They'd danced the night away, two young souls lost in love.

Suddenly inspired, Tom decided to recreate that night. He
wanted, if only for a few hours, to relive the spark of their early
days, to feel Eleanor's presence beside him once again.

The next evening, after dusting off their old record player and
digging out the Sinatra vinyl they'd danced to, Tom set the scene.

He laid out Eleanor's red dress on their bed, draped her pearls
beside it, and even placed her favorite red lipstick on the dresser.
The dining table was set with their best china, two candles
flickering in the center.

And then, in his best suit, Tom sat down with a plate of Eleanor's
favorite dish—spaghetti carbonara. The empty chair opposite him
wasn't truly vacant, he felt. Eleanor's laughter filled the gaps, her
memories kept him company.

After dinner, with Sinatra crooning in the background, Tom
danced. He held out his arms, picturing Eleanor in her red dress,

her head resting on his shoulder. They swayed together, lost in memories of their youth.

A soft knock interrupted his reverie. Opening the door, he found his granddaughter, Lily, eyes wide and curious. "Grandpa, what's going on?"

Tom smiled, brushing away a tear. "Just remembering a special night with your grandma. She loved dancing, just like you."

Lily grinned, holding out her hand. "Want to teach me?"

As they danced, Tom realized that while he missed Eleanor every day, their love was still alive—in the music, in the memories, and in the family they'd built. The evening wasn't just for him or Eleanor; it was a bridge to the past for Lily too.

When they finally rested, Tom pulled out the old photo album. Together, they laughed over memories and stories of the past. And as they turned the pages, there it was—a photograph of young Tom and Eleanor, radiant in her red dress, with Julia Roberts' same unmistakable smile.

88. Toy Story: Animation Like Never Before

The 90s was a time of innovation, and nothing exemplified it quite like "Toy Story"—the world's first fully computer-animated feature film. The rich details, the lifelike movements of toys, and the captivating storyline had everyone talking. It wasn't just a children's movie—it was history in the making.

In a small town, three generations—Grandma Rose, her son, David, and her lively granddaughter, Emma—decided to see the movie together.

They each had different reasons. For Rose, it was the memories of buying her son, David, his first toy cowboy. For David, it was the chance to relive the joys of childhood toys. And for Emma, well, she just wanted to see toys come to life!

The cinema was filled with the buzz of excited chatter. The lights dimmed, and the trio settled into their seats, their hands deep in tubs of buttery popcorn.

Rose watched with wonder. She remembered when animation was just pencil sketches on paper. But now, Woody and Buzz moved with such fluidity; they seemed almost real. The world had changed so much.

David was entranced by the storyline. He thought of his old toy box, tucked away in the attic, and wondered if his toys ever felt abandoned as Andy's did. The film was a bridge to his past, reconnecting him with memories long forgotten.

Emma's eyes sparkled throughout. For her, the magic was evident. She clapped, laughed, and gasped, utterly drawn into Woody and Buzz's adventures. Every scene was a marvel.

As they left the theater, Emma excitedly recounted her favorite parts, mimicking Buzz's "To infinity and beyond!" David shared stories of his favorite childhood toys, while Rose marveled at the incredible leap in animation.

Stopping at an ice cream parlor, David made a spontaneous decision. "Wait here," he said, disappearing only to return moments later with a toy cowboy and spaceman in hand. He passed them to Emma, "For new adventures," he smiled.

Rose took David's hand, squeezing it gently. The evening was more than just a movie. It was a reminder of the joy toys brought, the thrill of imagination, and the magic of storytelling.

89. Michael Jordan's Last Shot

The living room was awash in a golden hue, the remnants of the evening sun seeping in. On the couch sat Greg, in his mid-40s, right beside his 13-year-old son, Max.

Their attention was fixed on the old television set, tuning into one of the most anticipated basketball games of the decade: Michael Jordan's last game with the Chicago Bulls.

Greg remembered being Max's age, idolizing Jordan. He had posters, sneakers, and even once waited in line for hours, just to catch a glimpse of the basketball legend in person. Now, here he was, years later, sharing the magic of Jordan with his own son.

Max, in his Chicago Bulls cap—a hand-me-down from Greg—bit his nails, leaning forward. "Do you think they'll win, Dad?" he asked, eyes wide.

Greg chuckled, "With MJ on the court? Always believe."

The game was intense, with both teams locked in a fierce dance of offense and defense. Every shot, every pass felt momentous. But as the clock ticked down, the tension was palpable. It felt like the entire world was holding its breath.

Then it happened.

Jordan, with his signature flair, made a move that had the crowd roaring and the commentators shouting. The last shot. And it was nothing short of magnificent.

The room erupted. Greg whooped, and Max jumped, the two of them laughing and hugging, lost in the euphoria of the moment.

As the final cheers echoed from the TV, Greg reached for an old photo album from the shelf nearby. He flipped to a page showing a much younger him, donning a Jordan jersey, striking a similar pose to the legend himself.

"That's me, trying to be like Mike," he whispered with a grin.

Max laughed, "You looked cool, Dad!"

Greg playfully ruffled Max's hair, "Not as cool as you, champ."

The two settled back into the couch, surrounded by old jerseys, worn-out sneakers, and past game tickets strewn around the room—testaments to a long-held admiration. The world outside continued its pace, but inside that cozy room, time seemed to slow, encapsulated by the simple joy of a game well played.

90. The Mystique of Princess Diana

The scent of freshly baked scones wafted from the kitchen, drawing the Morgan family into the cozy dining area. It was their Sunday tradition to have breakfast together, followed by catching up on weekly news.

The newspaper lay open, the black and white image of Princess Diana, with that unmistakable gentle smile of hers, prominently featured. The headline read, "Remembering Diana: The People's Princess." It was the anniversary of her untimely passing.

Mrs. Morgan, with her reading glasses perched on her nose, began reading out the article detailing Diana's charitable works, her kindness, and her relentless passion for making the world a better place. The room was filled with a somber reverence, punctuated only by the gentle chime of the clock.

"I remember watching her wedding live," murmured Mr. Morgan, a hint of nostalgia evident in his voice. "The world was mesmerized by her, not just for her elegance but her genuine warmth."

Their teenage daughter, Lily, piped up, "At school, we learned about her campaign against landmines and how she visited hospitals secretly."

Young Timmy, just nine, looked puzzled, "Why was she so special, Mum?"

Mrs. Morgan smiled gently, "She had a way of making everyone she met feel seen and valued. Her kindness wasn't just for the cameras, Tim. She believed in it, lived it."

The family delved deeper into stories of Diana's charitable works, drawing inspiration from each tale. An idea began to form, taking root in the heart of each family member.

And so began the Morgans' new Sunday tradition. After their breakfast catch-ups, they would each perform a random act of kindness in honor of Diana. From baking extra scones for their elderly neighbor to volunteering at the local animal shelter, the Morgans found joy in giving.

One particular Sunday, Timmy handed Mrs. Johnson, their next-door neighbor, a bouquet of freshly picked wildflowers. Her eyes twinkled as she looked down at him, "What's this for, dear?"

"In memory of Princess Diana," Timmy replied earnestly.

Mrs. Johnson, touched by the gesture, simply replied, "She'd be proud."

Weeks passed, and the Morgans continued their acts of kindness. One Sunday, they found a note pinned to their front door. It read, "To the Morgan Family, thank you for your simple gestures. They remind us that love and kindness are always in season."

While they never discovered who left the note, they didn't need to. That small piece of paper, with its scribbled words, was a testament to the fact that the spirit of love and compassion, which Diana had championed, still resonated in the hearts of many, and could be rekindled with the smallest of gestures.

Every Sunday thereafter, the Morgans would smile at the note, which found a permanent spot on their fridge, a gentle reminder of the power of kindness.

91. Taking Flight with ValuJet

Mabel had lived 68 years without once stepping onto an airplane. The thought itself sent shivers down her spine. But this year, her grandchildren had moved to Florida, and the calls of "When are you visiting, Grandma?" became more frequent and pleading.

"Come by plane, Grandma! It's faster!" young Timmy would chirp.

Her daughter, Susan, encouraged her, "Mom, there's this new airline, ValuJet. It's affordable, and the service is great."

The intrigue of this new airline combined with the yearning to hug her grandchildren gave Mabel a renewed sense of purpose. She decided, after almost seven decades of feet firmly planted on the ground, to take to the skies.

Booking the ticket itself was an adventure. She painstakingly chose her seat, ensuring it was by the window, but not over the wings. "I want a clear view!" she declared to the amused ticketing agent.

The day arrived, and Mabel, donning her best dress and pearls, stepped into the airport. The hum of chatter, announcements over the PA system, and the occasional rumble of planes taking off filled the air. Her heart raced.

As she boarded ValuJet, the friendly stewardess, seeing her nervousness, whispered words of comfort. "You'll love it, promise. It's like floating on a cloud."

Mabel gripped her handbag as the plane sped down the runway, lifting gracefully into the sky. For the first time, she saw the world from above—the quilted fields, snaking rivers, and toy-like houses. The world felt vast yet incredibly connected. The nervousness melted away, replaced by awe.

After what felt like mere moments, the plane touched down in sunny Florida. As she disembarked, her grandchildren rushed towards her, their excited voices filling the air. "Grandma, you did it!"

Mabel hugged them tight, the exhilaration of her first flight still fresh. "Yes, I did. And I'd do it a thousand times over for these hugs."

Later that evening, as Timmy showed her his collection of toy planes, Mabel chuckled, "Next time, I might just pilot the plane myself!" The room echoed with laughter, the night etching itself as one of those precious memories, never to be forgotten.

92. Mall Walks and Food Courts

Every Saturday, precisely at 10 a.m., George and Martha would enter the bustling mall. But they weren't there for the shopping; they were there for their weekly "mall walk."

Clad in matching sneakers and fanny packs, the two would start from the south entrance, making their way through the maze of stores, smiling at familiar faces, and enjoying the medley of scents from perfume counters and the occasional hint of fresh popcorn.

Halfway through their walk, they'd reach their oasis: the food court. This wasn't just a pit stop for the couple. It was tradition. Sampling treats from various kiosks became their guilty pleasure. From teriyaki chicken at 'Oriental Delights' to those pretzel bites from 'Pretzel Palace', they reveled in the symphony of flavors.

Over the weeks, their little ritual caught the eye of fellow mall-goers. Clara, an elderly lady with a penchant for 'Pizza Corner' slices, started joining them.

Then came Bob, a widower, who swore by the hot dogs at 'Frank's Franks'. Before they knew it, George and Martha's duo turned into a lively group of six, all seniors, each with their food court favorite.

These "Food Court Friends," as they fondly called themselves, became inseparable. They'd share stories of bygone eras, of days when malls were a novelty and food courts a luxury.

Sometimes, they'd exchange tales of their youth, making younger eavesdroppers marvel at the history being narrated so casually over a shared plate of nachos.

One Saturday, the group decided to wear matching t-shirts with "FCF '92" printed on them. Mall regulars began to recognize them, with some even wanting to join the exclusive FCF club.

As the years went by, the mall underwent changes, but the Food Court Friends remained a constant.

Their laughter, infectious camaraderie, and love for mall delicacies became legendary. Young couples, teenagers, and even toddlers would wave and greet them, making the vast commercial space feel like a close-knit community.

For George and Martha, what started as a simple walking ritual transformed into a celebration of friendship, food, and reminiscing the good old days in the heart of the '90s mall culture.

93. The Magic of Harry Potter

It was a crisp autumn day in 1997 when Richard and Eleanor walked into the bookstore, searching for the perfect gift for their twin grandkids' tenth birthday. Eleanor, while adjusting her glasses, spotted a cover with a young boy, riding a broomstick. The title? "Harry Potter and the Philosopher's Stone."

"Harry who?" Richard muttered, skimming the blurb. Deciding it sounded delightful, they purchased the book, hoping the twins, Jenny and James, would enjoy the magical world they imagined it promised.

A week after the birthday, Jenny rang her grandparents. "Nana, Grandpa! This book is amazing!" she chirped. The excitement in her voice was palpable. James was equally smitten, declaring he was sure he'd be heading off to Hogwarts when he turned eleven.

Hearing such reviews, Eleanor's curiosity peaked. She decided to borrow the book. Each evening, she delved into the whimsical world of wizards, muggles, and magical creatures.

Eleanor was hooked. Richard, trying not to feel left out, insisted on reading it next. They spent evenings discussing the sorting hat's choices, the enigma that was Snape, and the bravery of young Harry.

Months passed, and as the world awaited the next Potter adventures, Richard and Eleanor found themselves queuing up with eager children (and many adults) at bookstores for midnight releases. They had cups of tea in mugs emblazoned with the Hogwarts crest and even contemplated making their own butterbeer.

The true magic, though, was the bridge the series built between them and their grandkids.

They'd discuss theories, debate on their favorite characters, and occasionally, Richard would attempt to craft wands in his woodworking shed. The twins, realizing their grandparents' newfound passion, gifted them robes one Christmas – Gryffindor for Eleanor and Hufflepuff for Richard.

The world of Harry Potter became a delightful escape and connection point for the entire family. Birthdays had themed cakes, and sometimes, the four would simply sit by the fire, reading the books aloud, each voicing different characters.

In a world that often revered the old and the new separately, the enchanting tales of a young wizard boy allowed Richard and Eleanor not only to revisit the wonder of childhood but also to share it intimately with the younger generation.

Magic, they learned, wasn't just in spells and potions, but in the shared experiences that spanned across ages.

94. The Y2K "Bug" That Wasn't

As the clock inched toward the new millennium, whispers of the Y2K bug grew louder. "Computers won't be able to handle the year 2000!" pundits cried.

From wild speculations about planes dropping from the sky to microwaves rebelling, it seemed like the apocalypse was nigh. The Johnson family, ever the cautious bunch, decided they weren't taking any chances.

Father Jack, a banker, meticulously printed out every family bank statement. "Just in case the electronic ones vanish!" he said with dramatic flair, earning an amused roll of eyes from his wife, Mary.

Mary, always the practical one, started her Y2K preparations in the kitchen. "We need to stock up," she declared, and soon enough, the pantry was full of canned beans, fruits, and vegetables. Enough, Jack mused, to last them a zombie apocalypse.

Teenagers Lisa and Rob saw a business opportunity. They went door-to-door, offering to "Y2K-proof" neighbors' computers for a nominal fee. Their method? Setting the system clock forward to January 1, 2000, and showing relieved homeowners that all was well when their screens didn't explode.

But the crown jewel of their Y2K preparations was Grandma Ellie's. Worried her beloved soaps would disappear with the televisions, she began recording every episode. By December, she had amassed hundreds of VHS tapes, all meticulously labeled.

New Year's Eve arrived, and the Johnsons, prepared for every eventuality, gathered in their living room. With a mix of excitement and apprehension, they counted down: "Five... Four... Three... Two... One!"

The clock struck midnight. The lights... remained on. The TV... continued broadcasting. The computer... hummed peacefully. The world... was just as it had been a second ago. There was a moment of stunned silence.

Then, little Rob broke the silence, "Can we open the beans now? I'm hungry."

Laughter filled the room. Jack leafed humorously through his printed bank statements, Mary opened a can of beans in dramatic fashion, Lisa and Rob high-fived for their "successful" business venture, and Grandma Ellie decided it was a good time to start her soap marathon.

The room filled with their collective laughter, a sound more vibrant than any New Year's celebration. Every year after, when New Year's approached, there was a playful debate in the

Johnson household: to prepare or not to prepare? But one thing was certain—they would always face the future, with its uncertainties and surprises, together.

95. The Swing Revival

The local community center had put up posters everywhere: "Swing Dance Night! Relive the '90s Revival!" Margaret and Richard exchanged amused glances when they saw it. The '90s swing revival? That made them chuckle. To them, the original era of swing in the 1940s was their golden period.

On the night of the event, Margaret donned a polka-dotted dress she'd kept since her younger days, and Richard managed to find his old two-toned shoes.

They arrived at the center to find a mix of generations. Young adults in zoot suits and fedoras swayed alongside older couples, the rhythm uniting all ages.

A live band struck up a familiar tune, and the wooden floor of the center vibrated with energy. As the opening notes of "Jump, Jive, an' Wail" played, the atmosphere was electric. Richard extended his hand, and Margaret, with a sparkle in her eyes, accepted. They might have been older, but their feet remembered every step.

Their movements were seamless, a dance they'd practiced and perfected years ago but never forgot. With every twirl and hop, they felt decades younger. Whispers spread around the room, and soon, a small crowd gathered, watching in awe.

The younger dancers, inspired by Margaret and Richard's grace, attempted to mimic their intricate steps.

When the song ended, the room erupted in applause. Margaret and Richard, a bit out of breath but glowing with happiness, took a bow. A young woman approached them, "That was incredible! Could you teach us some of those moves?"

Throughout the night, Margaret and Richard became the unexpected stars, teaching eager learners the original swing moves. By the end, the room was a swirl of polka dots, pin-up hairstyles, and joyous laughter.

As they left the community center, Margaret squeezed Richard's hand. "Who would've thought we'd be the life of the party in the '90s swing revival?" Richard chuckled, "It just goes to show, real swing never goes out of style."

With a shared smile, they walked into the night, their spirits as light as their dancing feet.

96. The Pokémon Card Trade

"Whatcha got there, Benny?" Grandpa Joe peered over his reading glasses as his young grandson, Benny, spread out an array of colorful cards on the living room table.

"Pokémon cards, Grandpa!" Benny exclaimed, holding up a shiny one. "This one's a Charizard. It's super rare!"

Grandpa Joe chuckled, a glimmer of nostalgia in his eyes. "You know, when I was your age, we traded baseball cards. Mickey Mantle, Joe DiMaggio... those were some of the big names."

Benny looked up with curiosity. "You traded cards too, Grandpa?"

"Sure did," Grandpa Joe replied, opening a drawer and pulling out a worn leather pouch. He gently laid out old, well-preserved baseball cards. The colors had faded, but the memories hadn't.

Benny's eyes widened. "Whoa! Are these valuable?"

"In money, maybe. In memories, definitely." Grandpa Joe smiled, pointing to one. "I traded three of my best cards for this DiMaggio."

Benny, intrigued, began asking questions. Which players were the fastest? The strongest? Who hit the most home runs? As

Grandpa Joe shared stories, Benny eagerly compared them to his Pokémon battles, drawing parallels between their two worlds.

It wasn't long before they hatched a plan. They'd set up a trading station at the next family gathering, where Benny's cousins would bring their Pokémon cards and Grandpa Joe's peers would bring their baseball cards. It would be a delightful exchange of stories and treasures across generations.

The day of the trade was filled with laughter, stories, and valuable lessons about the art of negotiation.

A cousin would passionately pitch the merits of a Jigglypuff, while one of Grandpa's friends would regale listeners about a near-miss at catching a foul ball from a legendary player.

As the sun set, Benny and Grandpa Joe sat back, a pile of new cards between them. The young boy looked at his grandfather, admiration in his eyes. "I think I like baseball cards too now, Grandpa."

Grandpa Joe ruffled Benny's hair, smiling warmly. "And I've got a soft spot for this Pikachu fellow. Funny how cards can bridge the gap between generations."

That night, Benny learned that while times change, the joy of collecting, trading, and sharing stories remains timeless.

97. The Pager: The Original Text Message

"Grandma, what's this?" Ellie held up a small, rectangular device she found in a dusty old box.

"Oh, my! That's a pager, sweetheart," Grandma Lucy said, her eyes lighting up with memories.

"A pager?" Ellie frowned, trying to find a screen or some buttons. "What's it for?"

Grandma Lucy chuckled. "Before smartphones and texting, dear, pagers were our lifelines. Someone would call a number, leave a short message or just their own number, and it would beep or vibrate to alert the person."

Ellie looked puzzled. "So, you had to find a phone to call them back?"

"Exactly! We'd rush to the nearest payphone or home phone to return the call," Grandma explained.

Uncle Jake jumped in, "I remember in high school, getting a page from your friends meant something cool was happening. We even had codes! '07734' meant 'Hello' if you looked at it upside down."

Ellie giggled, trying to visualize the number game. "That sounds fun! But also... a bit complicated."

Grandma Lucy nodded. "It was a simpler time, but it had its own charm. Your grandpa and I had our own little codes. A '143' from him meant 'I love you.'"

Ellie's eyes twinkled. "That's so romantic, Grandma!"

The family spent the afternoon sharing stories about the pager era. The rush to find a phone when the pager beeped, the joy of seeing a familiar number, and the occasional embarrassments like responding to a page while in the middle of a crowded mall.

As the sun began to set, Ellie pulled out her smartphone, "I just texted mom '143.' I think I'll make it our little code."

Grandma Lucy smiled, wrapping an arm around Ellie. "It's beautiful how some things, no matter how old or new, find a way to connect us all."

98. Coffee Shop Hangouts

Under the soft hum of coffee machines and amidst the warm aroma of freshly brewed coffee, a lively group of elderly friends had claimed a corner at the local "Bean N Brew." The '90s saw the rise of coffee shops as hangout spots, and while the world buzzed about the latest episodes of shows like "Friends," these older pals were crafting their own coffee shop tales.

Every morning at 9 am sharp, George, Lorraine, Harold, and Susan would convene. George, always punctual, would already be sipping his black coffee, no sugar, no cream.

Lorraine, with her love for cappuccinos, would be engrossed in the daily newspaper. Harold and Susan, always in sync, favored mochas with an extra shot of whipped cream. It wasn't just about the coffee, though; it was their ritual, their connection, a rekindling of their youth amidst the newer coffee culture.

The "Bean N Brew" became their sacred ground, echoing the warm, brick-walled coffee joints of sitcom fame. Here, stories were exchanged, from George's tales of his misadventures in the navy to Susan's vibrant recollections of the swing dances of her youth.

As they chatted, the world outside seemed to fade. The familiar chime of the door, the occasional steam release from the espresso machine, and their shared laughter created a world unto its own.

One chilly morning, the steam from their drinks merged with a soft golden sunlight filtering through the window, casting a hazy glow around them. The clink of Lorraine's spoon as she stirred her coffee, the rich scent of Harold's mocha, and the rustle of the morning paper held a certain kind of magic. At that moment, everything felt still. There was a shared, unspoken acknowledgment of the beauty in their simple routine.

The soft jazz track playing in the background seemed to resonate with their heartbeats, as they leaned into the comforting silence, each lost in their reverie, yet bound together by the heartwarming spell of the "Bean N Brew" mornings.

99. The Home Run Race

In the quiet suburbs of St. Louis, amidst the smell of freshly mown grass and the distant chatters of children playing, sat Frank's old armchair. It was positioned perfectly in front of the television, an oasis in the living room, where memories of grand slams and curveballs lingered.

Frank had lived a life enriched with the crack of bats, the cheer of crowds, and the fine dust of the diamond beneath his cleats.

Those days of playing minor league baseball felt like another lifetime, a collection of sun-soaked afternoons and electric nights under stadium lights. As age crept in, with its nagging knees and the occasional back pain, Frank's playing days faded, replaced by the monotony of retired life.

Then came the summer of '98.

As Mark McGwire and Sammy Sosa ignited the fields with their incredible home run race, a spark was rekindled in Frank. Each swing they took was a mirror, reflecting Frank's own youth, his dreams, and the sheer joy of the game.

The old radio in his garage, which had broadcast his minor league games, now echoed with the play-by-plays of these baseball titans. Every home run hit was not just a score on the board, but a journey back in time for Frank, each ball carrying fragments of his youth as it soared.

One evening, the neighborhood kids, having heard tales of Frank's baseball days, knocked on his door with a baseball and mitts in hand.

And there, in the gentle glow of twilight, with the chirp of crickets as the background score, Frank found himself teaching them the art of the perfect swing. Not as a former minor league player, but as a child of the game, his heart beating in rhythm with the thud of the ball against leather.

On the night McGwire hit his 62nd homer, surpassing Roger Maris, the entire neighborhood gathered in Frank's living room, eyes glued to the screen. The roar of the crowd, the jubilation—it was electric. Frank's eyes, however, were elsewhere, lost in the gleam of his old baseball trophy, basking in the golden hue of the television light.

That summer wasn't just about records and home runs. As the sun cast longer shadows on his lawn, Frank would often find himself on his porch, an old mitt in one hand, and a cool lemonade in the other.

The distant laughter of the neighborhood kids playing stickball, the familiar hum of the radio broadcasting another game, and the faint scent of his worn leather mitt - it was as if the universe had conspired to stitch together these moments, painting a canvas rich with hues of nostalgia.

And every time McGwire or Sosa sent another ball soaring into the stands, Frank felt it right in his chest, a palpable thump, like the gentle strumming of a well-loved guitar, resonating with the melodies of bygone summers.

100. Last Night at the Video Store

Martha's steps slowed as she neared the familiar storefront of "Rent-A-Flick." Its once bright neon sign now flickered intermittently, signaling the store's impending closure. The large "Closing Down Sale!" sign felt like a punch to the gut, making the ending all too real.

Pushing open the glass door, the familiar chime greeted her, instantly transporting her back to countless Fridays of her youth. The distinct aroma of buttery popcorn mixed with the faint scent of plastic cassette cases filled the air. It was the unmistakable smell of weekend anticipation.

Rows and rows of VHS tapes, each with its own story, beckoned her. Her fingers traced the spines as she walked down memory lane. There was the romantic comedy she and Jack had rented on their third date.

The horror movie that, much to her chagrin, she had to watch through her fingers, peering out from behind a cushion. And, of course, the numerous family movies with scenes her kids would reenact for days afterward, turning the living room into a stage.

In the kids' section, she smiled, recalling how her daughter, Lily, would pirouette, mimicking the ballerinas from her favorite musicals, while her son, Max, with a makeshift cape, would transform into the superheroes he idolized.

Those were the days when deciding on a movie could spark hour-long debates, usually ending in each child getting to pick one.

Paul, the ever-present store owner with an encyclopedic knowledge of films, looked up from the counter. Their bond was forged over shared film recommendations and critiques. "For the last time," Paul's voice broke the silence, his eyes reflecting a mix of sadness and fond remembrance.

She wandered over to the classics section, selecting a movie they had once passionately discussed. The same movie that sparked their first conversation, years ago.

Holding it up, she remarked, "For old times' sake?"

Paul smiled, nodding. "You always had impeccable taste."

As she approached the exit, she noticed a corner where Paul had set up a projector, playing snippets from classic films. The soft glow, combined with muffled dialogues, added to the store's charm.

Outside, the night air was crisp. Martha clutched her movie selection, a tangible piece of a bygone era. The world was changing, and while "Rent-A-Flick" might fade into history, the memories it housed, the weekends it shaped, and the stories it told would forever remain etched in the hearts of its patrons.

101. The Vinyl Revival

The attic had always been a place for forgotten memories and discarded heirlooms. Yet, today, as sunlight pierced through the cobweb-laden window, it shone upon a dusty corner holding old vinyl records. Jack, with silver hair cascading to his shoulders, gingerly approached them, hands trembling slightly.

He blew off the dust from a record cover, revealing a black-and-white image of a couple dancing. His fingers traced the silhouette of the woman, and memories flooded back.

He remembered a time when the living room was filled with melodies, when he and Lila would sway to the rhythm of love songs, her laughter echoing with the beat.

Taking a deep breath, Jack slowly lowered the needle onto one of the records. A soulful tune from the '70s filled the attic, every note tugging at his heartstrings. He closed his eyes, letting the music envelop him.

He remembered their first dance. Lila, with her raven-black hair flowing down her back, had an ethereal glow. They'd laughed at their clumsy moves, but as the night progressed, they danced as if they were the only two people in the world.

Jack's fingers tightened around a particular vinyl - their song. It was the tune they had danced to on their wedding day and on every anniversary that followed. Lila had always said, "Music is the thread that keeps our souls intertwined." And now, even in her absence, that thread felt stronger than ever.

Lost in the music, Jack began to move, his body recalling the familiar steps. Each spin, each sway was a tribute to the love they shared. The attic, with its forgotten memories, suddenly transformed into a ballroom of the past. And Jack, the solitary dancer, had an ethereal partner, dancing with him in his memories.

After what felt like hours, the music wound down, and the needle lifted from the record. Jack, with tears in his eyes, whispered, "For you, Lila." He felt a warmth, a presence, as if the room held not just music but echoes of a love that transcended time.

The attic, once a place of neglect, became Jack's sanctuary. He found himself visiting more often, playing different records, reliving memories. Friends and family began to notice the spring in his step, the joy in his eyes.

One day, his granddaughter, Emily, ventured up to the attic, having heard the distant music. She found her grandfather dancing, a big smile on his face. Intrigued, she approached the old record player, eyes wide with wonder. "What's this, Grandpa?"

Jack chuckled, "This, my dear, is the magic of vinyl."

He extended his hand, "Care for a dance?" Emily nodded enthusiastically, and they danced to tunes from a bygone era.

Over time the attic became a beacon of legacy. Neighbors, young and old, often heard melodies streaming down, enticing the curious to venture up. On weekends, it buzzed with children learning to dance, as Jack shared stories from each record.

While vinyl spun tales from a forgotten time, every note breathed life into the present. And there, amidst the melodies, the dance continued - a testament to timeless love and the lasting impression of music.

A Heartfelt Thank You

Dear cherished reader,

As we draw the curtains on this nostalgic journey through the decades, I want to take a moment to express my deepest gratitude to you. Your companionship along this voyage, page by page, has been the driving force behind these tales.

This book was crafted with love, care, and a deep respect for the memories that shape our lives. My hope is that these stories not only took you on a reminiscent trip down memory lane but also kindled warm conversations with loved ones, bridging the gap between generations.

If these tales brought joy to your heart and a smile to your face, I'd be immensely grateful if you'd consider leaving a review on Amazon. Your feedback not only helps others discover the stories but also guides me on future literary journeys.

Thank you once again for choosing to embark on this adventure with me. Wishing you countless moments of joy, laughter, and heartwarming memories.

With warmth and gratitude,
Alex

P.S. Every review, big or small, means the world to authors like me. If you enjoyed our time together in these pages, kindly drop a few lines on Amazon to share your experience.

Made in the USA
Las Vegas, NV
05 January 2024

83913251R00125